Alliances and International Relations

George Clarke
(Principal Teacher of Modern Studies)

Irene Morrison
(Principal Teacher of Modern Studies)

PULSE PUBLICATIONS

CONTENTS

Published and typset by
Pulse Publications
45 Raith Road, Fenwick,
Ayrshire, KA3 6DB

Printed and bound by
Ritchie of Edinburgh

British Library Cataloguing-in-Publication Data

A Catalogue record for this book is available from the British Library

ISBN 0 948 766 60 3

© Clarke & Morrison 1999
Reprinted 2001

TO THE TEACHER

Alliances and International Relations forms part of a series of books written for pupils studying Standard Grade Modern Studies. It is aimed at Foundation/General levels and concentrates on Syllabus Area 4.

The book has been designed and written as part of a course which will ensure that pupils are well prepared for the Scottish Qualifications Authority Standard Grade Modern Studies exams.

Throughout the book the activities concentrate on developing Knowledge and Understanding, but there are ample opportunities provided for pupils to develop enquiry skills. Each unit emphasises the concepts for Syllabus Area 4 – Need and Power. All Knowledge and Understanding activities are based around these concepts.

A 'What you will learn' box informs pupils of the main points to be learned from each unit.

A photocopiable Learning and Teaching Pack is available to accompany and enhance the use of this book. It contains:
- some important sources from the book to enable pupils to complete and retain their own copies
- map outlines
- succinct *revision notes*
- how to answer Knowledge and Understanding questions
- end of unit tests (KU and ES) at F and G levels
- overhead transparencies

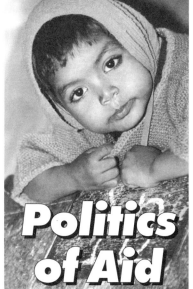

Politics of Aid

UNIT 1 – Rich world—Poor world

┌─ What you will learn: ─────────────────────────────┐

➤ That the world can be divided into 'rich' countries and 'poor' countries

➤ That there are many different names for 'rich' and 'poor' countries

➤ Which indicators show that a country is 'rich' or 'poor'

➤ The needs of people in 'poor' countries

└──┘

Concepts: NEED and POWER

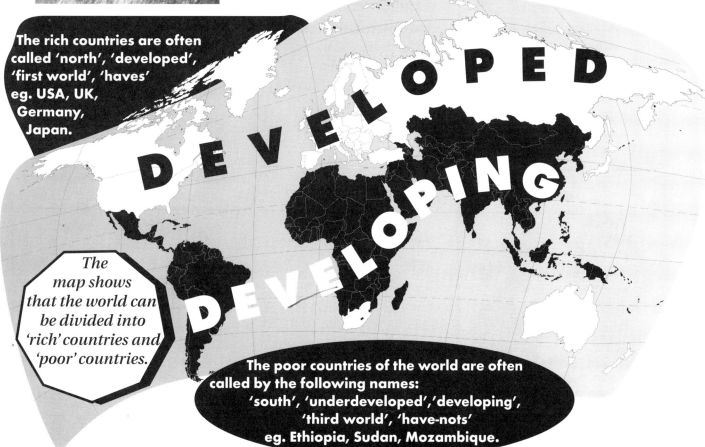

The rich countries are often called 'north', 'developed', 'first world', 'haves' eg. USA, UK, Germany, Japan.

DEVELOPED

DEVELOPING

The map shows that the world can be divided into 'rich' countries and 'poor' countries.

The poor countries of the world are often called by the following names:
'south', 'underdeveloped','developing', 'third world', 'have-nots'
eg. Ethiopia, Sudan, Mozambique.

In this part of the Standard Grade Modern Studies course, you will be finding out about what countries in the 'poor' world need and how these needs can be met with help from the 'rich' countries. For the purpose of this unit of work the 'poor' countries will be referred to as 'developing' countries and the 'rich' countries will be referred to as 'developed' countries.

ACTIVITIES

Copy the heading: **The Politics of Aid**
Copy out the 'What you will learn' box.
1 Read carefully all of the information above.
   a) On a blank map of the world, shade in the developed and the developing countries of the world.
   b) Give your map an appropriate key and heading.
2 Copy the table below and put the words in the correct column.

Words used for developed countries	Words used for developing countries
developed	developing

have-nots   rich   underdeveloped   haves   poor   first world   north   third world   south

3

'HAVES AND HAVE-NOTS'

Judith from the UK

School

Television and computer games

Leisure time

Food

ACTIVITIES

1 Look carefully at the picture of Judith from the UK and the drawings around this page.

In the middle of the paper you are working on, write down a description of Judith. Round about your description, either write or draw the things that Judith probably has eg. nice clothes. Underneath all of this, write out the things that she might not have. Your page should look like this.

happy ☺

Judith
• lives in the UK
• is rich
•
•

nice clothes

Judith does not have
•
•
•

2 Repeat this activity for Haile from Ethiopia.

3 Write a paragraph comparing what sort of lives Judith and Haile might have.

Medicine

Clean water

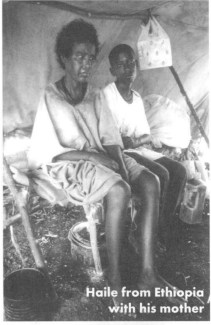
Haile from Ethiopia with his mother

Shelter

Transport

Cooking

Holidays

● Birth rate is the number of babies born for every 1,000 people in a country. In Ethiopia the birth rate is 47. This means that for every 1,000 people in Ethiopia 47 babies are born. The higher the birth rate the poorer the country is.

● Death rate is the number of deaths for every 1,000 people in a country. The death rate in the UK is 11. This means that for every 1,000 people in the UK 11 die. The higher the death rate the poorer the country is.

● Infant mortality rate is the number of babies who die before they reach their first birthday out of every thousand who are born. In Ethiopia, 127 babies die before they reach their first birthday for every 1,000 who are born. The higher the infant mortality rate the poorer the country.

● Life expectancy is the average number of years newborn babies can be expected to live if health conditions stay the same. The lower the life expectancy the poorer the country is.

● Urban/rural population: if a country has a high percentage of people living in the countryside (rural) then it is a developing country.

● Population per doctor: in Ethiopia there is one doctor for every 88,150 people. The higher the number of people per doctor the poorer the country is.

● Literacy rate is the percentage of people over 15 who can read and write a simple letter. The lower the literacy rate the poorer the country is.

● GNP: Gross National Product is the value of a country's goods and services divided by its population. The higher the GNP the richer the country is.

COMPARING A DEVELOPED COUNTRY AND A DEVELOPING COUNTRY

	Profile of a developing country – Ethiopia in 1993 –	Profile of a developed country – The UK in 1993 –
Total population (in millions)	57	57
Birth rate (per 1,000)	47	14
Death rate (per 1,000)	20	11
Infant mortality rate (per 1,000)	127	7
Life expectancy (years)	46	76
Urban/rural population(%)	14/86	90/10
Population per doctor	88,150	680
Literacy rate (%)	18	99
GNP ($)	120	12,000

Factfile: Africa

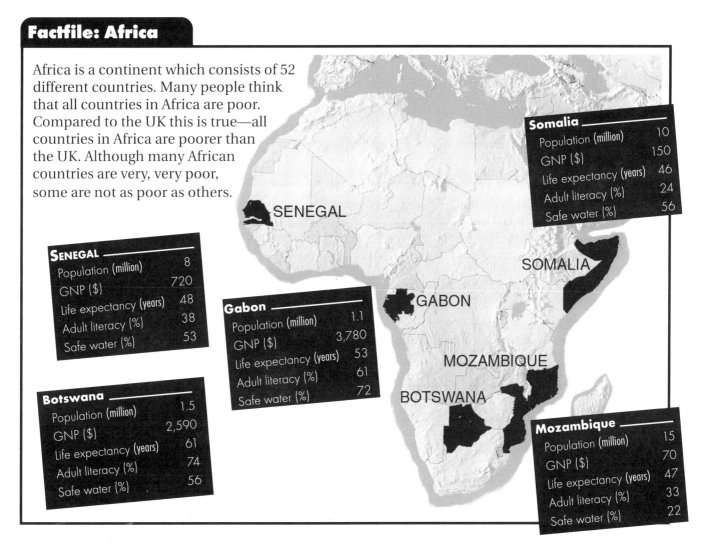

Africa is a continent which consists of 52 different countries. Many people think that all countries in Africa are poor. Compared to the UK this is true—all countries in Africa are poorer than the UK. Although many African countries are very, very poor, some are not as poor as others.

Somalia
Population (million)	10
GNP ($)	150
Life expectancy (years)	46
Adult literacy (%)	24
Safe water (%)	56

SENEGAL

SOMALIA

Senegal
Population (million)	8
GNP ($)	720
Life expectancy (years)	48
Adult literacy (%)	38
Safe water (%)	53

GABON

Gabon
Population (million)	1.1
GNP ($)	3,780
Life expectancy (years)	53
Adult literacy (%)	61
Safe water (%)	72

MOZAMBIQUE

Botswana
Population (million)	1.5
GNP ($)	2,590
Life expectancy (years)	61
Adult literacy (%)	74
Safe water (%)	56

BOTSWANA

Mozambique
Population (million)	15
GNP ($)	70
Life expectancy (years)	47
Adult literacy (%)	33
Safe water (%)	22

ACTIVITIES

Study the information on page 5.

1 Using either the word 'high' or the word 'low' copy and complete these sentences.

   In a developed country such as the United Kingdom,

   • the birth rate is ....

   • the death rate is ....

   • the infant mortality rate is ....

   • life expectancy is ....

   • the rural population is ....

   • population per doctor is ....

   • the literacy rate is ....

   • the GNP is ....

   In a developing country such as Ethiopia,

   • the birth rate is ....

   • the death rate is ....

   • the infant mortality rate is ....

   • life expectancy is ....

   • the rural population is ....

   • population per doctor is ....

   • the literacy rate is ....

   • the GNP is ....

2 Name one African country which is very poor. Explain how the figures in the Factfile helped you to decide this.

3 Name one African country which is not so poor. Explain how the figures in the Factfile helped you to decide this.

4 Make up a poster with the title 'Rich world/poor world'.

5 Learn the words and meanings from the Keywords box.

6 Make up a sentence which shows the meaning of the following words. Here is an example.

Word:	*developed*
Sentence:	The UK is a *developed* country which means that it is a rich country.

Words: *developing*

birth rate

life expectancy

GNP

KEYWORDS

developed:	A rich country like the United Kingdom where most people work in manufacturing industry and service industries.
developing:	A country where most people work in agriculture. It is trying to become a developed country.
urban:	Things to do with towns and cities
rural:	Things to do with the countryside
continent:	A large area of land with many countries eg Africa

Enquiry Skills

INVESTIGATING USING A CD-ROM

You are investigating a developing country in Africa. You are going to use a CD-Rom to gather information. A CD-Rom is an encyclopaedia on a Compact Disk. It contains writing, photographs, videos and sound. There are many CD-Roms which will have information on developing countries in Africa eg. *National Geographic Magazine* and *The World Guide.*

Using a CD-Rom to investigate has some good points and some bad points.

GOOD POINTS

- They contain large amounts of information—thousands of newspapers can be stored on one CD-Rom.
- You get typed information, photographs, diagrams, video and sound clips.
- They can be cheap to use, particularly if borrowed from the library. Computer magazines sometimes give away free CD-Roms.
- They are easy to use.

ACTIVITIES

Copy the heading: **Enquiry Skills – Investigating using a CD-Rom**

1 What is a CD-Rom?

2 Why is using a CD-Rom a good way to investigate a developing country in Africa?

3 Copy the statements below about using a CD-Rom. Beside each statement write down whether it is a good point or a bad point.

- *They are easy to use.*
- *If you do not have a computer with a CD player you cannot use a CD-Rom. They are expensive.*
- *The information is not updated so it can quickly become out-of-date.*
- *Large amounts of information – thousands of newspapers can be stored on one CD.*
- *You get typed information, photographs, diagrams, video and sound clips.*
- *Some CD-Roms are difficult to search.*
- *They can be cheap to use, particularly if borrowed from the library. Computer magazines sometimes give away free CD-Roms.*
- *It can be difficult to get the information you want because there is so much information on a CD-Rom.*

BAD POINTS

- It can be difficult to get the information you want because there is so much information on a CD-Rom.
- If you do not have a computer with a CD player you cannot use a CD-Rom. They are expensive.
- The information is not updated so it can quickly become out-of-date.
- Some CD-Roms are difficult to search.

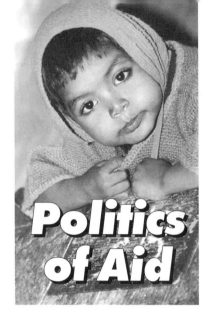

Politics of Aid

What you will learn:

➤ The main problems facing developing countries in Africa

➤ How to interpret a bar chart

➤ How to interpret a cartoon

Concepts: NEED and POWER

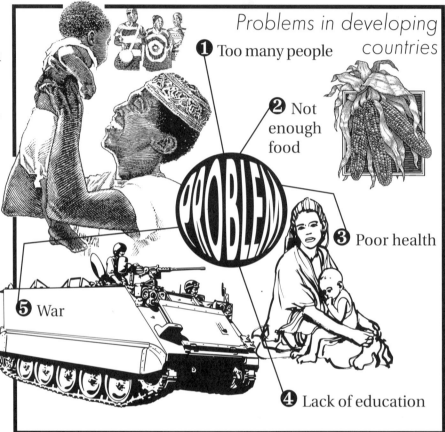

Problems in developing countries

❶ Too many people

❷ Not enough food

PROBLEM

❸ Poor health

❺ War

❹ Lack of education

Many developing countries in Africa suffer from a series of problems which makes life very difficult. These problems are all linked to each other.

PROBLEM 1
TOO MANY PEOPLE

The population of the world in 1990 was 5,000 million (5 billion) people. Figure 2.1 shows the world's population in a bar chart.

It is estimated that by the year 2025 the total population of the world will be 8 billion with 1 billion in the developed world and 7 billion in the developing world. This means that all the population increase will be in the countries of the developing world. In 1990 the number of people in the developed countries was 1 billion. By 2025 there will still be 1 billion people in these countries.

This bar chart shows the population of the world in 1990. It shows 3 main things:

1 In 1990 the total population of the world was 5 billion people.

2 In 1990 the developed countries had 1 billion people.

3 In 1990 the developing countries had 4 billion people.

This is an example of one way in which you can *interpret* a bar chart.

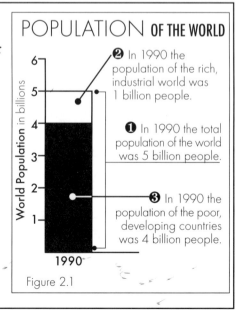

POPULATION **OF THE WORLD**

❷ In 1990 the population of the rich, industrial world was 1 billion people.

❶ In 1990 the total population of the world was 5 billion people.

❸ In 1990 the population of the poor, developing countries was 4 billion people.

World Population in billions

1990

Figure 2.1

ACTIVITIES

Copy the heading: **Problems facing developing countries in Africa**

Copy the 'What you will learn' box.

1 In your own words, say what are the main problems facing countries in Africa.

2 Copy out the heading: **Problem 1: Too many people**

Draw your own bar chart to show the population of the world in 1990 and how it was distributed between the developed and the developing countries.

3 Now add to your bar chart the estimated population of the world in 2025 and how it will be distributed between the developed and the developing countries.

4 Try to interpret this bar chart. Look back at Figure 2.1. Write down at least 3 things that this bar chart tells you.

5 Write down 3 things which Figure 2.2 tells us about population in the United Kingdom.
   • population in 1993
   • population in 2025
   • size of the increase

6 Write down 3 things which Figure 2.3 tells us about population in Ethiopia.

7 What conclusions can you come to about population in developed countries like the UK compared to population in developing countries like Ethiopia? (Look at the 2 bar charts and your interpretation of them.)

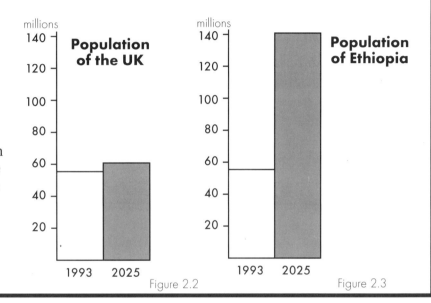

Figure 2.2

Figure 2.3

PROBLEM 2
NOT ENOUGH FOOD

ACTIVITIES

Copy the heading:
Problem 2 – Not enough food

1 Study the cartoon opposite.

   Describe, in detail, what the cartoon is telling you about the population and food in the world in 1993.

2 Copy and complete the sentences using the words below.

The cartoon shows a map of the ...... in the year ...... It is divided into ...... and .... The north has lots of ...... but not a lot of .... The south has not a lot of ...... but lots of ....

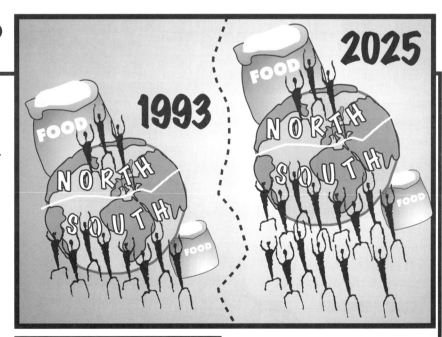

WORDS TO USE:
north food world people
food people 1993 south

3 Explain, in detail, what the cartoon is telling you about the population and the food in the world in 2025.

WHY IS THERE NOT ENOUGH FOOD?

According to some experts, not enough food means eating fewer than 2,200 calories a day. Calories are the energy you get from food. The map shows the parts of the world which have enough food and those which do not have enough food.

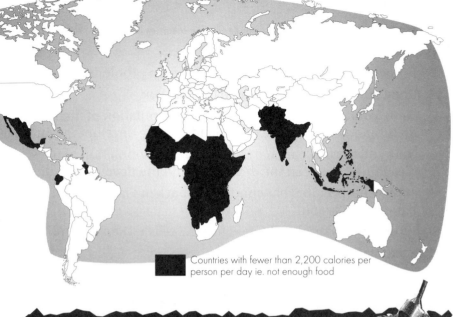

■ Countries with fewer than 2,200 calories per person per day ie. not enough food

As you can see, all the countries which do not have enough food are in the part of the world with the developing countries. Most of the countries in Africa do not have enough food.

● Dependence on cash crops
These are crops which are grown to make money and not to feed the people. For example, cotton is a cash crop in Ethiopia. Much of the good land is used to grow cotton and the farmers cannot grow food to feed their families. These crops are used to pay off the country's debt.

LACK OF FOOD CAN BE CAUSED BY ....

● War
Many countries in Africa are at war—either with another country or a civil war. The land is devastated by fighting and many of the farmers have to fight in the war. It is difficult to move food from one part of the country to another because the roads are blocked and the lorries get blown up.

● Too much debt
This means that the farmers have to grow crops which the government can sell to pay off its debt. The people starve in the meantime.

● Too many people living on the land
This means that the land will not grow enough food to feed all the people.

● The climate is too hot, cold, dry or wet
This means that it can be difficult to grow crops.

● Diseases and pests can kill animals and crops
Diseases such as sleeping sickness can kill cattle while pests like locusts can destroy crops.

● Poor soil
The soil can be poor because:
- it can be over-farmed and this c[an] turn the land into desert
- it is too high up—i[n] the mountains maybe

● Poor farming methods
Ways of farming the land can be poor because:
- the farmers are illiterate
- the bits of land are very small
- they either have no machinery or it is out-of-date or it has broken down and they cannot get the part they need to fix it
- they cannot afford fertilisers.

10

Copy out the heading: **Why is there not enough food in some countries in Africa?**

1 What is the minimum number of calories needed each day for a person to survive?

2 What is a calorie?

3 Get a blank map of the world. Colour in the areas of the world which have fewer than 2,200 calories a day. Give your map an appropriate key and title.

4 According to the map, do most people in Africa have enough food to feed themselves?

5 Look at the section 'Lack of food can be caused by...' on page 10.
   Explain why there is a lack of food in some countries in Africa.

PROBLEM 3
POOR HEALTH

People who do not get enough food can fall ill more easily. They can suffer from *undernutrition* or *malnutrition*.

Undernutrition means that you do not get enough of any type of food.

Malnutrition means that you do not get enough of the right types of food. It comes from the French—bad eating. Many people in developing countries suffer from malnutrition. This can lead to a number of diseases and illnesses such as kwashiorkor and marasmus.

Measles is a killer in developing countries. In the UK when children get the measles, they suffer from a high temperature and get a rash for a day or two and then they recover. Very few die.

In developing countries, measles can affect whole populations. Many will remain ill for a long time and thousands will die slowly. This is partly because their resistance is low because they do not get enough food and partly because they cannot get the medical help they need.

Factfile: Health in developing countries

WHY DO PEOPLE IN DEVELOPING COUNTRIES HAVE POOR HEALTH?

In developing countries many people do not get medical help when they are ill.

Fact 1   They might live many miles away from the nearest doctor. This might be as many as 100 miles away. They would have to walk to the surgery.

Imagine if you were ill and had to walk 100 miles for treatment.

Imagine you had to go to the doctor and there was a queue of 1,000 people waiting to see her. How many pupils are there in your school? This might give you an idea of how long you would have to wait.

Fact 2   In developing countries such as Ethiopia there is only one doctor for every 88,150 people.

Fact 3   In most developing countries there is no health service run by the government. You would have to pay the doctor before she would look at you.

You check his pulse, I'll check his wallet.

Imagine you earned £5 a week but the doctor charged £10 to look at you.

Fact 4   Any medicines usually have to be paid for. Many medicines we take for granted are not available or cost a lot of money.

Imagine the doctor prescribed a course of antibiotics. They are only available in the nearest hospital which is over 700 miles away and they will cost you £150.

Copy out the heading: **Problem 3: Poor health**

2 What is the difference between undernutrition and malnutrition?

3 What happens when there is an outbreak of measles in a developed country like the UK?

4 What happens when there is an outbreak of measles in a developing country like Ethiopia?

5 Why is there such a difference between measles in the UK and measles in Ethiopia?

6 Study the pictograph below.

What does the pictograph tell you about health in the UK compared with Ethiopia?

7 Write a paragraph to say why people in developing countries like Ethiopia have difficulty getting medical help when they are ill.

PROBLEM 4
LACK OF EDUCATION

Education is an important part of people's lives. If you cannot read and write you will be unable to do lots of things. Imagine you got a new computer game for Christmas. Without the written instructions, it could take you forever to work out how to load the game. What use is a game you cannot play?

Being able to read and write is important. If people could not read and write then there would be no doctors, no car mechanics, no TV repair people, no newspapers or magazines. Imagine life without medical help, without transport, without TV, videos or computers.

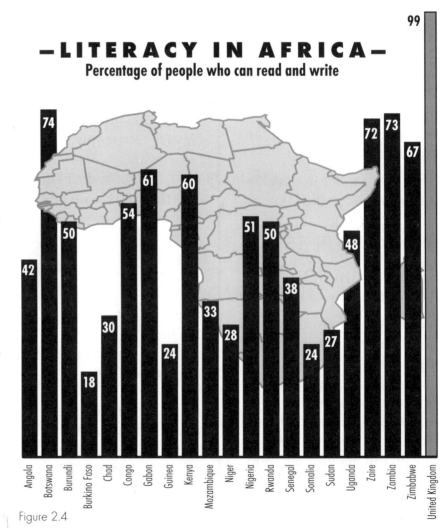

—**LITERACY IN AFRICA**—
Percentage of people who can read and write

Angola 42, Botswana 74, Burundi 50, Burkina Faso 18, Chad 30, Congo 54, Gabon 61, Guinea 24, Kenya 60, Mozambique 33, Niger 28, Nigeria 51, Rwanda 50, Senegal 38, Somalia 24, Sudan 27, Uganda 48, Zaire 72, Zambia 73, Zimbabwe 67, United Kingdom 99

Figure 2.4

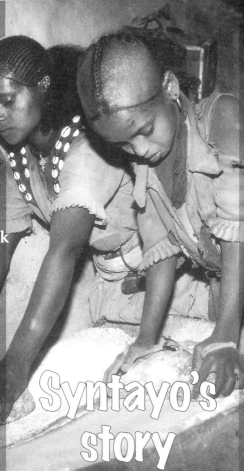

Syntayo and her brother Tesfai live in Ethiopia. They live in a village. Syntayo is fifteen and she is about to be married. She cannot read or write.

She was taught by her mother to look after the house, to cook, to clean, to sew, to gather firewood, to carry water and how to look after her younger brothers and sisters.

Her parents thought that these were the skills she would need to attract a good husband. Her life would be to look after her husband's home, help in the fields and bring up his children. It was not important for her to learn to read and write.

Tesfai is two years younger than Syntayo. He has learned to read and write and count. He left school a year ago to help his family herd the cattle. He reads to his family in the evening. He reads them the leaflets about personal hygiene, about using clean water, about being inoculated and about how to improve their farm.

He is very well respected by other people in his village because he can read so well and is so young. Some villagers think he should go to Khartoum and learn to become a teacher or a doctor so he can come back and help the village.

Syntayo's story

WHY IS THERE A LACK OF EDUCATION IN SOME AFRICAN COUNTRIES?

There are two main reasons why there is a lack of education in some African countries.

- Lack of money for teachers, equipment and schools
- Differences in the way men and women are treated in some African countries

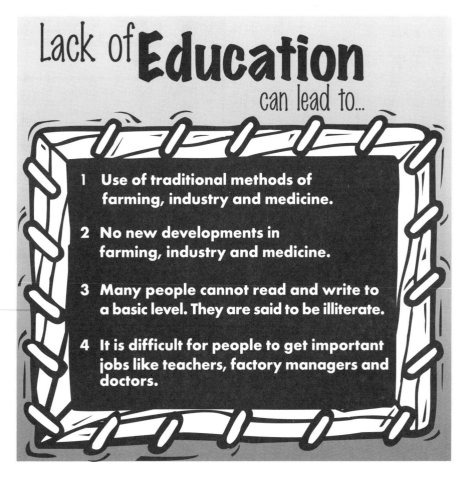

Lack of **Education** can lead to...

1 Use of traditional methods of farming, industry and medicine.

2 No new developments in farming, industry and medicine.

3 Many people cannot read and write to a basic level. They are said to be illiterate.

4 It is difficult for people to get important jobs like teachers, factory managers and doctors.

Copy out the heading: **Problem 4: Lack of education**

1 Why is education important?

2 Look at the Figure 2.4 on page 12. It shows the percentage of people who are literate in some developing countries in Africa. Which of these statements are true according to the graph? Copy out the true ones only.

   – *Less than half of the people in Angola are literate.*

   – *More than half of the people in Botswana are literate.*

   – *More people in Zaire than in Kenya can read and write.*

   – *Less than half of the people in Congo are literate.*

   – *More than half of the people in Kenya are literate.*

   – *More people in Gabon than in Congo can read and write.*

   – *Less than half of the people in Mozambique are literate.*

   – *More than half of the people in Zambia are literate.*

   – *More people in Uganda than in Sudan can read and write.*

3 Why might a lot of people in Somalia, for example, not be able to read and write?

4 Copy and complete this diagram to show the effects a lack of education can have on a country and its people. The missing words are in the Missing Words box. This diagram can be called a spider diagram. It is a good way to make notes on a topic. This type of diagram can be used to help you to revise or to plan an answer in an exam.

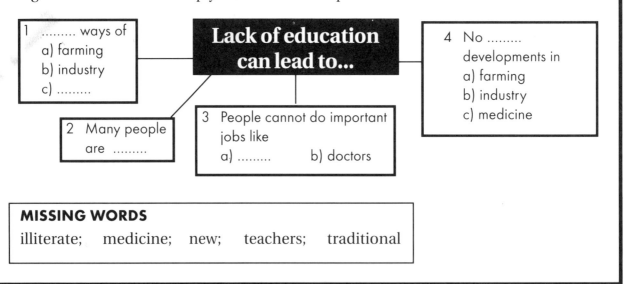

1 .... ways of
  a) farming
  b) industry
  c) ....

Lack of education can lead to...

4 No ....
developments in
  a) farming
  b) industry
  c) medicine

2 Many people are ....

3 People cannot do important jobs like
  a) ....   b) doctors

MISSING WORDS

illiterate;   medicine;   new;   teachers;   traditional

KEYWORDS

antibiotics	drugs which help to cure people from diseases
civil war	a war between two or more groups in one country
convoy	a group of vehicles travelling together
debt	owing money
dependence	relying on something
fertilisers	chemicals which are used to improve the amount of crops grown
GNP	Gross National Product – the total amount of goods produced in a country. The wealth of a country.
illiterate	unable to read and write

WARS IN AFRICA

Wars use up badly needed resources. Instead of spending money on things they need, countries often spend money on weapons. For example, in Sudan when there was a famine in 1991, the government sold all of the country's grain to pay for weapons.

SPENDING BY 3 AFRICAN COUNTRIES AS A PERCENTAGE OF THEIR GNP

% of GNP

ETHIOPIA — Military, Health, Education
SUDAN — Military, Health, Education
SOMALIA — Military, Health, Education

Figure 2.5

NIGERIA 1967–1970

SUDAN 1985–1995

ETHIOPIA 1974–1979

UGANDA 1971
RWANDA 1991
BURUNDI 1991

ZAIRE 1960–1965

ANGOLA 1961–1995

ZIMBABWE 1961–1995

MOZAMBIQUE 1981–1989

The Effect of War on a Developing Country

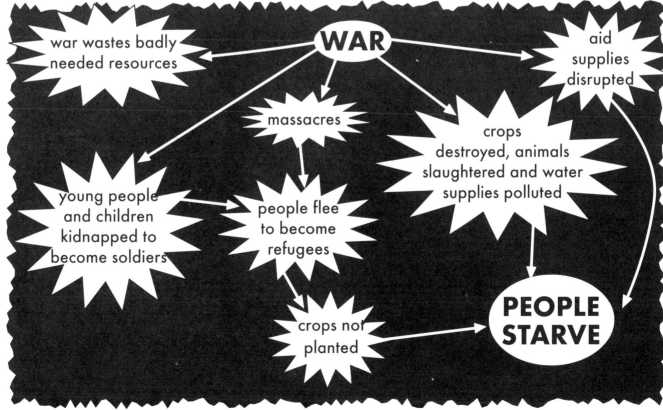

WAR

war wastes badly needed resources

aid supplies disrupted

massacres

crops destroyed, animals slaughtered and water supplies polluted

young people and children kidnapped to become soldiers

people flee to become refugees

crops not planted

PEOPLE STARVE

Case Study: *The effects of war on Nyareth from Sudan*

Nyareth lived in a village in Sudan. It was in the middle of a war. Her husband joined the rebels. The army attacked the village. They burned the crops and killed all the cattle to stop the rebels from getting supplies. They took her 2 older sons away to become soldiers. One boy was 11 and the other was 13.

The people of the village did not plant any seeds. What they had they needed to eat. Anyway, the soldiers would have come back and burned their fields.

The village elders heard that there was a food convoy coming to a camp in the area. All 50 people in the village began to walk to try to find the food. After 2 days, they found a refugee camp and waited for the food convoy. 15 of the villagers had died during the walk. Nyareth had 3 young children with her. One died from diarrhoea within 5 days of reaching the camp.

She got very little food for herself and her children. The aid convoys are often stopped by the army or the rebels. Nyareth stayed at the camp and would not return to the village until she could live with her children in safety and plant her crops in peace.

ACTIVITIES

Copy out the heading: **Problem 5: War**

1 Collect a blank map of Africa. Colour in and label your own map showing some of the main wars in Africa. Give your map an appropriate key and title.

2 Find out more about one of these wars. Write your notes up as a report.

3 Look at Figure 2.5 which shows spending by some African countries as a percentage of GNP.

   a) What is meant by GNP?

   b) For each country, write a short paragraph, describing what the bar chart tells you.

   c) What conclusions can you come to about the importance to countries like Ethiopia of military spending compared with spending on health and education?

4 Produce one of the following to show the effects of war on a developing country in Africa and its people:
poster, newspaper article, report, talk or OHP presentation to the class.

5 Learn the words and meanings in the Keywords boxes on page 14 and below.

KEYWORDS

kwashiorkor	disease caused by a lack of protein in the diet. Symptoms are swollen belly and poor growth.
marasmus	disease caused by a lack of calories in the diet. Symptoms are people are very thin—'skin and bone'.
massacre	to slaughter a large number of people
rebels	people who fight against the government
refugees	people who are fleeing from war or famine
traditional	the way things have always been done

Politics of Aid

UNIT 3 – Problems need Solutions!

What you will learn:

➤ Aid is given to help developing countries to meet their needs

➤ There are different types of aid

➤ Why countries give aid to other countries

Concepts: NEED and POWER

Developing countries in Africa have 5 main problems. Study the information in the table below.

PROBLEM	NEED	SOLUTION
1 Too many people	To control population growth	Improve primary health care
2 Not enough food	To grow more food; to have more food supplies	Encourage farmers to use their land properly
3 Poor health	Water; medicine; education; good food	Get clean water supplies
4 Lack of education	Schools; teachers; equipment; equality for women	Train teachers; build schools
5 War	Peace; security	Get help from the United Nations

HOW CAN THE WORLD HELP TO SOLVE THESE PROBLEMS?

Countries of the world and some organisations like the United Nations can help to meet the needs of developing countries in Africa by giving them *aid*. A country which gives aid is called a donor country. A country which gets aid is called a recipient country.

WHAT IS AID?

Aid is help given by a country or organisation to another country to help it to meet its needs. For example, Ethiopia needs water. The United Kingdom can help to meet this need by giving Ethiopia equipment to drill wells.

✏ ACTIVITIES

Copy the heading: **Problems need solutions**

Copy the 'What you will learn' box.

1 Fit the phrases below into the spaces in the paragraph to make up a note about needs and solutions. Give the paragraph a suitable title.

Developing countries in Africa have 5 main problems. The first one is that .... It is therefore necessary to .... This can be done by ....

The second problem is that not enough food is grown. It is necessary to .... This can be done by ....

The third problem is that people suffer from poor health. It is therefore necessary to get .... This can be done by ....

The fourth problem is that there is not enough .... To solve this problem it is necessary to ....

The fifth problem is .... A solution to this problem is to ....

- improving primary health care
- grow more food
- get help from the UN
- education
- train teachers
- encouraging farmers to use the land properly
- there are too many people
- control population growth
- medicine and water
- getting clean water supplies
- war

WHAT ARE THE DIFFERENT TYPES OF AID?

☆ BILATERAL AID

This is aid given directly from one country to another.
(bi=two; lateral=sides; bilateral=two-sided ie. from one country to another)

☆ MULTILATERAL AID

This is aid given to a country by an organisation such as the United Nations (UN). The UN collects money from rich countries. The UN then gives aid to developing countries in Africa. For example, Sudan needs schools. The UN builds schools in Sudan. The people of Sudan can then learn to read and write.

☆ VOLUNTARY AID

Charities such as Oxfam, Save the Children, Christian Aid and SCIAF collect money from the people in rich countries. The charities then use the money they collect to give aid to developing countries in Africa. The money can be collected in a number of ways such as collecting cans, charity shops and television appeals.

ACTIVITIES

Copy the heading: **How can the world help to solve these problems?**

Carefully read the information under this heading.

1 Make your own notes on aid and types of aid. You can use a spider diagram to help you to do this.

What is aid?   Bilateral Aid

TYPES OF AID

Voluntary Aid   Multilateral Aid

18

WHAT ARE THE MAIN FORMS OF AID?

Bilateral aid, multilateral aid and voluntary aid can be given to the recipient countries in a number of different forms.

EMERGENCY AID
✳ war
✳ famine
✳ earthquake
✳ flood
✳ drought
✳ failed harvest

When a country is hit by one or more of these problems, aid has to be sent in fast to save lives. This is called emergency aid. This is short-term aid.

MILITARY AID
🔫 guns
🔫 tanks
🔫 helicopters
🔫 military advisers

Military aid is given to a country when we want it to be on our side and also to support governments we approve of.

DEVELOPMENT AID
➕ technical help eg. tractors, water pumps
➕ advisers eg. crop experts, mechanics
➕ volunteers eg. teachers, doctors, nurses

Development aid is long-term aid given to help a country overcome its problems and to improve its standard of living. It helps the people to help themselves.

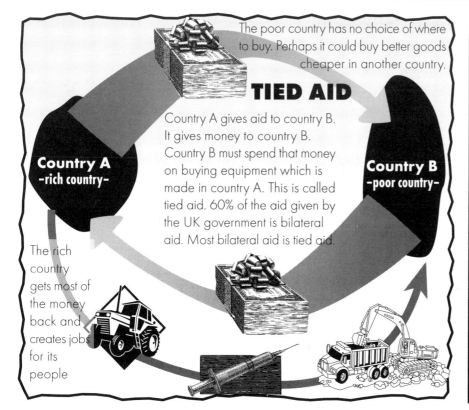

The poor country has no choice of where to buy. Perhaps it could buy better goods cheaper in another country.

TIED AID

Country A gives aid to country B. It gives money to country B. Country B must spend that money on buying equipment which is made in country A. This is called tied aid. 60% of the aid given by the UK government is bilateral aid. Most bilateral aid is tied aid.

Country A
–rich country–

Country B
–poor country–

The rich country gets most of the money back and creates jobs for its people

ACTIVITIES

Copy the heading:
What are the main forms of aid?

1 Copy these sentences.

   Bilateral aid, multilateral aid and voluntary aid can be given in a number of different forms. The main forms are: emergency aid, military aid and development aid.

2 For each of these forms of aid (emergency aid, military aid and development aid)
   a) explain what is meant by that form of aid;
   b) give at least two examples of the ways that aid can be given.

3 "Most bilateral aid is tied aid." Explain, in detail, what this means.

BILATERAL AID – THE ODA IN AFRICA

The ODA was the part of the government which looked after aid. Its aim was to help poor people in poor countries. In 1997, after the General Election, the ODA disappeared and a new department was set up called the Department for International Development (DFID).

BRITISH AID TO MOZAMBIQUE

British aid has tried to help Mozambique improve its economy. Britain has provided spare parts, raw materials and equipment. Vital transport links have been reopened. Emergency relief has been given to refugees.

● Britain has provided help to set up courses in English language.

● Aid has been given to provide spare parts and replacement machinery for British made electricity generators in Mozambique power stations.

● Britain provided new port handling equipment and helped rebuild a jetty for handling oil products.

● Britain has provided road construction and bridge building experts so that the main roads in Mozambique could be rebuilt.

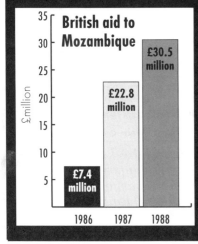

British aid to Mozambique

- £7.4 million (1986)
- £22.8 million (1987)
- £30.5 million (1988)

Since 1983 all bilateral aid to Mozambique from the ODA has been given as grants. This means that Mozambique does not have to pay the money back.

● Up to 1989, Britain provided £14million to help rebuild the Limpopo railway. After 1989, Britain provided another £15million to build more track and bridges.

WHY DO COUNTRIES GIVE AID?

We give aid for *political* reasons.
We like to help countries where we approve of their style of government.
We like to help countries which we want to have on our side.
We like to help countries which have governments that believe in capitalism.

We give aid for *social* reasons.
We want to help people who are poorer than we are.
We want to help them develop their own country.
We want to put an end to hunger, disease and illiteracy in the developing countries of Africa.

We give aid for *economic* reasons.
We help countries which trade with us.
We help countries because they will buy goods from us and so keep our workers employed.

What's in it for them?

ACTIVITIES

Copy out the heading: **Why do countries give aid?**

1 Study the diagram British Aid to Mozambique.

   Give examples of ways in which Britain has given bilateral aid to Mozambique.

   Make notes to help you learn these examples. You can use a spider diagram.

2 Write out these 3 headings at the top of three columns.

For social reasons	For political reasons	For economic reasons

Put the following statements under the appropriate heading.

● to help people who are poor

● to help countries which trade with us

● to help stop hunger and disease

● to help countries which have democratic governments

● to help countries so that they will buy goods from us

● to help countries which we want on our side

Politics of Aid

UNIT 4 – The United Nations and its agencies – multilateral aid

┌─ What you will learn: ─────────────────────────────────┐

➤ What the main specialised agencies of the United Nations are

➤ How the United Nations tries to improve the lives of people in the developing world

└──┘

Concepts: NEED and POWER

LOGO	NAME OF SPECIALISED AGENCY	AIM OF UN AGENCY	HOW THE AGENCY HELPS DEVELOPING COUNTRIES
	World Health Organisation (WHO)	*To help improve health*	● To help countries build up their own health services especially primary health care ● To run campaigns to wipe out diseases such as TB, measles, tetanus etc.
	Food and Agricultural Organisation (FAO)	*To reduce hunger and to improve food supplies*	● To help train people to improve their farming methods by developing irrigation schemes, good crop management, use of pesticides
	United Nations Children's Fund (UNICEF)	*To meet the needs of the poorest children in the poorest countries in the world*	● To give help to children during/after disasters ● Works with WHO to run health programmes such as immunisation against measles
UNESCO	United Nations Educational Scientific and Cultural Organisation	*To improve education*	● To teach basic reading/writing skills ● To train teachers ● To build schools

🖌 ACTIVITIES

Copy out the heading: **The UN and its agencies – multilateral aid**

Copy out the 'What you will learn' box.

1 Make up your own FactFile on UN agencies by matching up one piece of information with each of the four boxes opposite.

2 Look carefully at the logo of the FAO. Describe what the logo shows. Try to find out what *fiat panis* means.

> HOW IT HELPS DEVELOPING COUNTRIES
>
> LOGO
>
> NAME OF UN SPECIALISED AGENCY
>
> AIM OF UN AGENCY

United Nations Children's Fund

United Kingdom Committee for UNICEF
55 Lincoln's Inn Fields, London WC2A 3NB

UNICEF is one of the agencies of the United Nations. It acts on behalf of children in developing countries.

- It is concerned with the main causes of death and disease among children under 5.
- It is concerned with making sure that girls are given their basic rights.
- It is concerned with fighting disease, malnutrition and poverty which kill 35,000 children every day.

Examples of how UNICEF meets the needs of developing countries in Africa

To help children to read and write UNICEF gives
- textbooks
- pencils
- rulers
- paper
- crayons

To help young people earn a living UNICEF gives
- hammers and saws
- cows
- sewing machines
- microscopes

To help children get the food they need UNICEF gives
- fish
- carrots
- chickens
- seeds
- hoes

To help keep children healthy UNICEF gives
- immunisation
- stethoscopes
- bandages
- medicines
- water pumps

What UNICEF spends its money on

- community based services for women and children 7%
- child nutrition 4%
- education 10%
- water supply and sanitation 11%
- project support 15%
- child health 31%
- emergency aid 22%

The UK Committee for UNICEF contributed £6,079,500 to help children in 32 countries

Ethiopia £60,000: UNICEF has helped by providing clean water, medicine and food for children in refugee camps.

Somalia £1,191,000: Water systems were repaired, 75 wells were dug, 650,000 children under five were vaccinated against measles.

Botswana £35,000: In co-operation with WHO, UNICEF helped to set up local health services.

Mozambique £270,000: Helped with water supplies, sanitation and health education.

15,000 children in the developing world die every day from diarrhoea. To be more accurate, they die from dehydration caused by diarrhoea. The main causes of diarrhoea are poor hygiene and lack of clean drinking water. Diarrhoea leads to malnutrition. Malnutrition leads to dehydration. The child actually dries up and may be dead within hours. Diarrhoea is difficult to treat. It can be done through improving water supplies and immunising children against diseases such as measles. However dehydration must be treated fast. This can be done in a very simple way—by oral rehydration therapy (ORT). This means giving the child a mixture to replace the water and salt which the body has lost. By mixing water, salt and sugar in the right proportions, the child rehydrates and, within one hour, can return from the brink of death.

Oral Rehydration Therapy

1 teaspoon of salt
1 litre of clean water
8 teaspoons of sugar

Serve at regular intervals and save a child's life

Eleven ways UNICEF helps children with just £1

£1 = A foetal stethoscope to monitor heartbeats before birth.

£1 = Enough high dose vitamin A capsules for 30 toddlers to be protected against nutritionally caused blindness for one year.

£1 = Enough antibiotic ointment to treat six children afflicted with trachoma, an eye disease which, if left untreated, can lead to blindness.

£1 = Enough vaccine to immunise 20 children against tuberculosis.

£1 = Enough vaccine to immunise 15 children against the triple threat of diphtheria, whooping cough and tetanus.

£1 = A vaccine storage thermometer for monitoring vaccine storage temperatures.

£1 = Two clinical thermometers for a health centre.

£1 = Enough Piperazine tablets to cure over 25 children suffering from intestinal worms.

£1 = Three bottles of chloroquine syrup to treat children suffering from malaria.

£1 = Exercise books for 10 children.

£1 = A pound of pea seeds or six packets of lettuce seeds for a school or community vegetable garden.

Copy the heading: **United Nations Children's Fund – UNICEF**

1 Using the words from the wordbox, copy and complete the following paragraph.

WORDBOX • children • countries • die • food • future • health care
• school • need • read • ill • write • water

UNICEF cares for ...... everywhere. Children ...... good ...... , clean ...... and .... Without these children become ...... and sometimes they .... Children also need to go to ...... to learn to ...... and ...... so that they can have a better .... UNICEF helps developing ...... to provide all these things for their children.

2 Read these four sentences carefully. Using the pie chart on page 23, write out the two which are correct.

   a) UNICEF only spends 22% of its money on emergency aid.

   b) UNICEF spends a high percentage of its money on education.

   c) UNICEF spends the highest percentage of its money on child health.

   d) Water supplies and sanitation are important to UNICEF. It spends half of its money on this.

3 Write a paragraph explaining how UNICEF helps to meet the needs of developing countries in Africa.

Copy the heading: **An example of a campaign by UNICEF to try to improve the health of children**

4 Why might children die if they get diarrhoea?

5 What is ORT?

6 Explain how oral rehydration therapy (ORT) can prevent children from dying from diarrhoea.

Enquiry Skills

INVESTIGATING USING THE INTERNET

You are investigating the work of UNICEF. You are going to use the internet to gather information. The internet links millions of computers around the world using telephone lines. UNICEF has its own website which has large amounts of information about its work. Using the internet to investigate has some good points and some bad points.

GOOD POINTS

✔ Large amounts of up-to-date information on all subjects.

✔ Able to get information from most countries in the world.

✔ You get typed information, photographs, diagrams, video and sound clips.

✔ It can be cheap to use if you do not spend too much time on-line.

✔ You can get information very quickly.

✔ You can use e-mail to talk to other people on the internet and get answers to the questions you want to ask.

BAD POINTS

✘ If you spend too long on the internet you will have a large telephone bill.

✘ The internet has information which is unsuitable eg. people may put in lies or their own opinions which are not always true.

✘ It can be difficult to get the information you want because there is so much information on the internet.

✘ If you do not have a computer and a telephone you cannot use the internet.

✘ Computers are expensive.

✘ Looking at a screen for too long can lead to health problems.

ACTIVITIES

Copy the heading: **Enquiry Skills – Investigating using the internet**

1 What is the internet?

2 Why is the internet a good way to investigate the work of UNICEF?

3 Copy the statements below about using the internet. Beside each statement write down whether it is a good point or a bad point.

- Large amounts of up-to-date information on all subjects.
- If you spend too long on the internet you will have a large telephone bill.
- It can be difficult to get the information you want because there is so much information on the internet.
- You can get information very quickly.
- You get typed information, photographs, diagrams, video and sound clips.
- If you do not have a computer and a telephone you cannot use the internet.
- It can be cheap to use if you do not spend too much time on-line.
- The internet has information which is unsuitable eg. people may put in lies or their own opinions which are not always true.

WORLD HEALTH ORGANISATION

+ WHO says that health is "the state of complete physical, mental and social wellbeing and not just about being ill."

+ Poor h-ealth is connected to poverty, lack of good food, dirty water, no sanitation and poor housing.

+ WHO set targets for the developing world to reach by the year 2000.

   ◉ to raise life expectancy from 56 to 65

   ◉ to reduce infant mortality by 50%

   ◉ to end malnutrition

   ◉ to immunise all children against the six killer diseases:

     ✟ diphtheria

     ✟ TB

     ✟ polio

     ✟ tetanus

     ✟ whooping cough

     ✟ measles

Factfile: Killer diseases

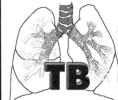

TB (tuberculosis) is a lung disease which is spread by coughing or drinking infected milk. It spreads quickly when people live in overcrowded conditions.

cough! cough! cough!

Whooping cough has serious effects on children in developing countries. Young babies often die. It is spread by coughing.

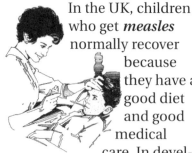

In the UK, children who get **measles** normally recover because they have a good diet and good medical care. In developing countries measles often causes blindness or death.

Polio is caused by a virus which is found in food or water. It attacks children who can be left paralysed or who may die.

Tetanus infection enters the body through a cut. It can cause death.

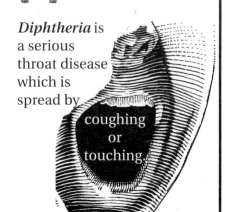

Diphtheria is a serious throat disease which is spread by coughing or touching

ACTIVITIES

Copy the heading: **The World Health Organisation – WHO**

1   WHO has set targets to improve health by the year 2000.

   a)   One of its targets is to raise life expectancy. What is meant by life expectancy?

   b)   WHO wants to reduce infant mortality by 50%. Explain what this means.

   c)   WHO wants to end malnutrition. What is meant by malnutrition? (See page 11.)

   d)   WHO wants to immunise all children against the 6 killer diseases. What are the 6 killer diseases?

   e)   Write a sentence about each of the 6 killer diseases.

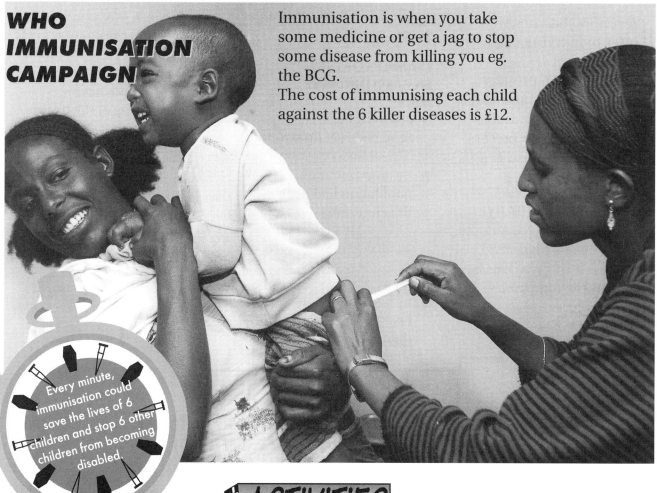

WHO IMMUNISATION CAMPAIGN

Immunisation is when you take some medicine or get a jag to stop some disease from killing you eg. the BCG.

The cost of immunising each child against the 6 killer diseases is £12.

Every minute, immunisation could save the lives of 6 children and stop 6 other children from becoming disabled.

SUCCESS OF THE CAMPAIGN

● 80% of children in the world were immunised against the 6 diseases by the end of 1990.

● This has saved 3 million lives and prevented 50 million cases of measles each year.

ACTIVITIES

Copy the heading: **WHO immunisation campaign**

1   Look carefully at the cartoon of the stop watch. What is the cartoon telling us?

2   What is meant by immunisation?

3   How successful has the campaign been so far?

People who live in rural areas of developing countries in Africa cannot get to a hospital easily when they are ill. For example, in Tanzania only 5% of people live near a hospital. If people cannot get to the health care, the health care must be taken to the people.

Preventing bad health is better than trying to cure it.

The purpose of primary health care is to take health care to the people and to educate people to prevent them from getting diseases such as measles etc.

THE BAMAKO INITIATIVE

WHO and UNICEF set up a new project called the Bamako Initiative. This is an example of primary health care.

AIM OF THE BAMAKO INITIATIVE

Health services are set up in the local communities in the country instead of in the big cities.

WHO IS TAKING PART?

Twenty two countries in Africa are participating in this initiative. So far 2,000 health centres have been set up, taking medical services to over 20 million people in Africa.

EXAMPLES OF THE BAMAKO INITIATIVE

Benin

● 200 local health centres have been set up covering 57% of the population

● By June 1993, 86% of the population had been given BCG immunisation and 71% had been immunised against polio.

Guinea

● In 1987 there were only 31 health centres and fewer than 5% of the children were immunised.

● In 1993 there were 265 health centres and more than 76% of the children had been immunised.

HOW SUCCESSFUL HAS THE BAMAKO INITIATIVE BEEN?

✔ The quality of health services has improved.

✔ More people are being immunised.

✔ Money is saved because people in the country areas do not have to travel so far to health centres.

✔ Local people have a say in the running of the health services.

ACTIVITIES

Copy the heading:

WHO – Primary Health Care Project

1 What is meant by primary health care?

2 Read the information on the Bamako Initiative.

Write a short report on the Bamako Initiative.

Use the headings below to help you.

REPORT ON BAMAKO INITIATIVE
– AN EXAMPLE OF
PRIMARY HEALTH CARE –

● AIM OF THE INITIATIVE

● EXAMPLES OF THE INITIATIVE

● SUCCESSES OF THE INITIATIVE

FOOD AND AGRICULTURAL ORGANISATION (FAO)

STREET FOOD

One of the projects supported by the FAO to improve the diet of people in the developing countries of Africa is 'street food'. Street food is ready to eat food sold on the streets of the cities in the developing countries of Africa.

There is one main problem with street food. It is not hygienically prepared and can lead to illness.

To improve street food three main things are needed.
– Clean water
– Garbage disposal
– Training in preparing food

The FAO helps to set up training workshops to teach the people about preparing food. It also advises the people who buy the food about which foods are healthy and which are not.

ACTIVITIES

Copy the heading; **Food and Agricultural Organisation – FAO**

1   Make notes on street food and what the FAO is doing.

Copy and complete the spider diagram to help you to make your notes.

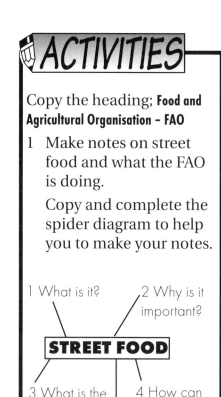

1 What is it?

2 Why is it important?

STREET FOOD

3 What is the problem with street food?

4 How can street food be improved?

5 What is the FAO doing to help?

- In Senegal in 1979 50,000 people made and sold street food.
- Street food is food grown by local farmers.
- It is mostly women who prepare and sell street food. Many of these women are illiterate.
- Street food is very important as it feeds hundreds of millions of people.
- Many poor people who live in cities depend on street food as their main source of cooked food. Many of these people live in shanty towns and have no cooking facilities.

UNESCO A SCHOOL IN A SUITCASE

Here is an example of the type of aid UNESCO is offering Rwanda to help it to rebuild its education system after the 1991 civil war.

Before the 1991 civil war and the genocide in 1994, Rwanda had a good education record. More than 60% of children went to primary school. However, only 6% of these children ever went on to secondary school.

After the killings in 1994, many of the teachers had been killed and the school buildings had been destroyed. UNESCO has tried to help by handing out 'school in a suitcase' packs. These are emergency classrooms inside a suitcase. In the case are 80 slates, rubbers, chalks, exercise books, blackboard paint, alphabet cloths, wall hanging multiplication tables and even Scrabble type games to play. UNESCO has shipped in 9000 suitcases and trained a group of teachers to use them.

ACTIVITIES

Copy the heading: **United Nations Educational, Scientific and Cultural Organisation – UNESCO**

Read the story 'A school in a suitcase'.

1   Write your own story about the work UNESCO is doing to help Rwanda to rebuild its education system.

2   Draw a poster showing a suitcase. In the suitcase draw and name all the things that are needed to make up a school.

WATERAID – AN EXAMPLE OF VOLUNTARY AID

Factfile: Water

* Water is a basic necessity for life.
* The average amount of water used by someone in the UK each day is 130 litres.
* The average amount of water used by someone in Africa each day is 10 litres.
* In Africa, women spend 3 to 4 hours per day collecting water.
* More than a billion people in the world have no access to clean water.
* Only 19% of people in Ethiopia have access to clean water.
* 80% of all disease is caused by dirty water including
  - diarrhoea
  - malaria
  - typhoid
  - cholera
* Half the hospital beds in Africa are occupied by people suffering from diseases caused by dirty water.

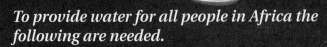

To provide water for all people in Africa the following are needed.

- *appropriate and inexpensive technology*
- *education and training*
- *local community involvement*

ACTIVITIES

Copy the heading: **Voluntary aid – WaterAid**

Read the Factfile on water.

1 From the list below, copy out the *true* statements and *rewrite* the ones which are false so that they are true.

  ● Everyone needs water to survive.

  ● People in Africa, on average, use more water than people in the UK.

  ● Women, in Africa, spend about 4 hours every day collecting water.

  ● Fewer than a quarter of the people in Ethiopia can get clean water.

  ● More than 1,000 million people do not have access to clean water.

  ● Most diseases are caused by dirty water.

  ● Diarrhoea is not linked to dirty water.

  ● Not many people are in hospital with diseases which they have got because of dirty water.

2 People in Africa need clean water. What can be done to help make sure they get clean water?

3 Describe and explain what the cartoon is trying to say.

4 Make up your own cartoon about Africa and water.

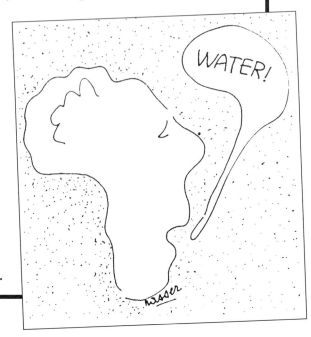

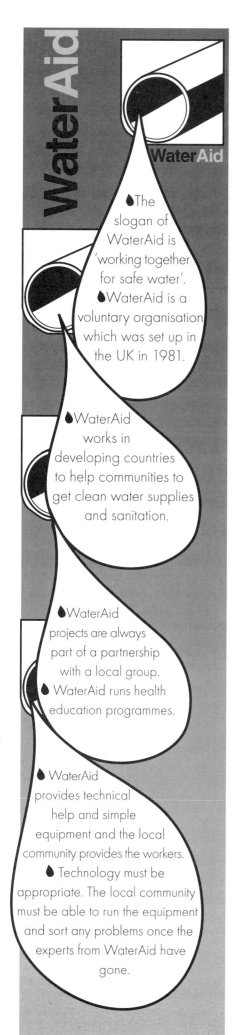

- The slogan of WaterAid is 'working together for safe water'.
- WaterAid is a voluntary organisation which was set up in the UK in 1981.
- WaterAid works in developing countries to help communities to get clean water supplies and sanitation.
- WaterAid projects are always part of a partnership with a local group.
- WaterAid runs health education programmes.
- WaterAid provides technical help and simple equipment and the local community provides the workers.
- Technology must be appropriate. The local community must be able to run the equipment and sort any problems once the experts from WaterAid have gone.

–CASE STUDY–
WATERAID IN KENYA

Mwanaisha Mweropia, a 23-year-old mother of six from Kinaini in Kenya used to make seven journeys in the hot sun each day to get water. There was always a queue at the well. No one was allowed to fill more than one bucket at a time. She was always tired.

Her life was changed because of WaterAid. WaterAid, working with the Kenyan Water for Health Organisation (KWAHO) and the people of Kinaini, brought a clean water supply to her village.

In 1988 the people of Kinaini set up a water committee. They raised £250 to get a survey done to see what their water needs were. Plans were drawn up for a new water supply. The community wanted to do the work but they did not have the equipment or the skills.

In 1991, WaterAid provided money for equipment for the project. They sent experts to train the local people to build and look after the water supply. The whole community worked together to complete the project. They piped safe, clean water into their community and built toilets to prevent the water supplies from being contaminated. WaterAid ran workshops for women on basic health care.

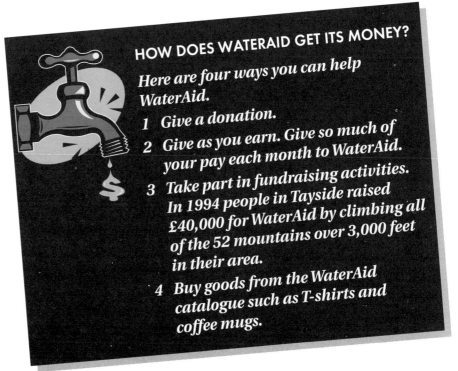

HOW DOES WATERAID GET ITS MONEY?

Here are four ways you can help WaterAid.

1. Give a donation.
2. Give as you earn. Give so much of your pay each month to WaterAid.
3. Take part in fundraising activities. In 1994 people in Tayside raised £40,000 for WaterAid by climbing all of the 52 mountains over 3,000 feet in their area.
4. Buy goods from the WaterAid catalogue such as T-shirts and coffee mugs.

1 Look carefully at the WaterAid information on page 31. Here are some questions and answers about WaterAid. They are mixed up. Unjumble them to make up a set of questions and answers about WaterAid. Try to put them in a logical order – an order that leads from one point to the next.

QUESTIONS

1 What does WaterAid hope to do?
2 What is the logo for WaterAid?
3 Why must the technology used be appropriate?
4 What is the slogan of WaterAid?
5 When and where was WaterAid set up?
6 In which countries does WaterAid work?
7 What else does WaterAid do?

ANSWERS

● WaterAid's slogan is 'working together for safe water.'
● WaterAid works in developing countries.
● WaterAid was set up in 1981 in the UK.
● The technology must be appropriate because the local people have to be able to use the equipment.
● WaterAid runs health education programmes.
● WaterAid aims to get clean water and sanitation to communities.
● The logo of WaterAid is a pipe with a big drip coming out.

2 Explain, in your own words, how WaterAid helped Mwanaisha Mweropia.

3 Design a leaflet showing how people can help WaterAid to get its money.

APPROPRIATE AND INAPPROPRIATE AID

Appropriate aid is aid which improves the lives of people in a country. It has to be aid which the people can use and understand. It has to be aid which they can fix if it breaks down.

Inappropriate aid is aid which makes life worse for people. It is aid which leads to them losing their land or their jobs. It is aid which they do not understand or cannot use because it is too expensive.

EXAMPLES OF INAPPROPRIATE AID

Western governments asked the Bedouin what they wanted most and were told water for the camels. Wells were dug and plenty of water was provided. The camel herds multiplied, but there was not enough food for them all. Many died and the Bedouin were left with fewer camels than they started with.

Yugoslavia built a factory in Ghana for canning mangoes. The factory was able to put more mangoes into cans than were grown in the whole world.

The USSR built a milk bottling factory in Sudan. People in Sudan do not like milk from bottles. The factory has been built for over 25 years and has never made one bottle of milk.

In Senegal, the USA built silos for wild grain. They cost $2 million. They were built in places where the people do not go so they have never been used.

The great groundnut scheme: A lot of money was spent trying to grow groundnuts in Tanzania. People lost their land. Tractors were used to do the work so there were no jobs for people. The groundnuts would not grow in Tanzania.

ACTIVITIES

Copy the heading:
Appropriate and Inappropriate aid

1 What is meant by appropriate aid?

2 Why are the following examples of aid not appropriate? Choose a reason from the list.

AID

1 Groundnut scheme in Tanzania.

2 Silos built to store wild grain.

3 Milk bottling factory in Ghana.

REASONS

1 Grain silos were built in the wrong place.

2 The crop would not grow in that country.

3 The people did not like milk in bottles so the factory was never used.

ACTIVITIES

Copy the heading:
Military Aid v Development Aid

1 Study the cartoon 'Tanks or Village Development' and the information box.

Why do you think the cartoon shows tanks knocking down houses, a village clinic and a school?

2 Copy and complete the diagram opposite.

Factfile: Military Aid

→ Military aid makes a country poor.

→ Arms sales to the developing world represent over 60% of the world's sale of weapons.

→ Most developing countries spend more on defence than they do on education and health care.

→ Estimates suggest that the money spent throughout the world every two weeks on weapons could provide everyone in the world with adequate food, water, education, health and housing.

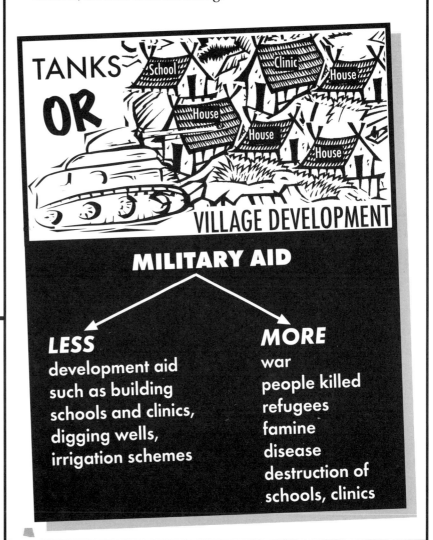

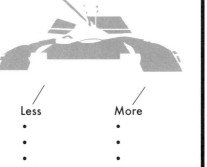

RICH COUNTRIES CAN GIVE AID OR TAKE IT AWAY

Namari is a developing country. Namari has a very poor education system. Only 32% of its people can read or write. The UK government gives Namari £32 million of aid to improve its primary education system.

In Namari there is a company called OIL (UK). It is drilling for oil and causing a great deal of pollution in the marshlands along the coast. The new government of Namari tells OIL (UK) to stop polluting the marshlands as this is poisoning the fish and the people there cannot live without fishing.

OIL (UK) says it cannot afford to put in all the equipment needed to stop the pollution. The Namari government then orders OIL (UK) to stop drilling for oil until it cleans up the way it works.

The British government cancels the £32 million of aid for education in Namari until the government allows OIL (UK) to continue drilling for oil.

RICH COUNTRIES CAN DECIDE TO BUY GOODS OR THEY CAN REFUSE TO BUY GOODS

Maranawi is a developing country. Maranawi has very little industry. It depends on buying modern machinery and goods from the rich countries. Maranawi people once grew crops to feed themselves although they were very poor.

The Maranawi government was persuaded that it would be good for the country to grow cotton. They could export the cotton and they could buy food for the people. There would be money left over to modernise the country.

The government made the farmers grow cotton. For a while they made money from selling the cotton to the rich countries. They bought food for the people and they began to buy modern machinery to improve the country.

The government of Maranawi changed. The rich countries did not like the new government. The rich countries stopped buying Maranawi's cotton. Now the people are starving.

RICH COUNTRIES HAVE STRONGER ARMIES

The government of Ghataar was run by the army generals. The people were poor and the generals kept control by using the army to terrorise the population. Ghataar had lots of oil and the generals used the money from the oil to buy weapons.

Eventually a civil war broke out. Despite having powerful weapons the generals were defeated because many of their soldiers turned against them. They fled over the border with their followers.

After an election the government took control of all the oil production. They began to sell oil to buy food for the people and to rebuild the roads, the houses, the schools and the clinics.

The old generals and their followers invaded the country. They had been given new weapons by a powerful rich country. A civil war broke out between the generals' army and the people's army.

The rich powerful country invaded. It said it was there to stop the civil war. It landed thousands of soldiers and there were two aircraft carriers full of modern jet fighters lying off the coast. They brought in modern tanks.

Very soon the rich country's soldiers were in control of the main cities and the members of the new government were arrested.

New elections were held. The old generals were elected. They gave back control of oil production to the companies which were there before. When their army was strong enough, the powerful country withdrew its army and said that there was now peace in the country.

POWER

ACTIVITIES

Copy the heading: **Rich countries have power over poor countries**

1 Why did the UK give aid to Namari?
2 Why did the UK cancel the aid to Namari?
3 Imagine you were a member of the Namari government.
   Read the statements which follow. Copy the one you agree with.

   "I would refuse to allow OIL (UK) to continue to pollute the marshland."

   "I would allow OIL (UK) to start drilling for oil again."

   Give one reason to support your decision.
4 What will happen because of your decision?
5 Read the two statements and answer the question which follows.

   "The UK has power over the government of Namari."
                          – statement A

   "The UK has no power over the government of Namari."
                          – statement B

   Which statement do you agree with?
   Give one reason from the source to explain your answer.
6 Describe two other ways in which rich countries have power over poor countries.

The United Nations

What you will learn:

➤ That the United Nations helps to meet the defence needs of Europe by keeping the peace

➤ Why there has been fighting in Bosnia

➤ How the United Nations (and NATO) tried to stop the war in Bosnia

Concepts: NEED and POWER

WHAT IS THE UN?

The United Nations is a world organisation which tries to:

● prevent war

● stop war once it has started

● help the victims of war

WHAT CAN THE UNITED NATIONS DO?

It may take any of the actions shown below. The Security Council is the part of the United Nations which decides what to do. The Security Council has fifteen members.

Help! The Omegans are attacking us. Call the UN to stop the fighting.

How can you help us?

ALPHALAND

OMEGALAND

The UN in Action

PEACEKEEPING FORCE
UN soldiers are invited into a country to stop the two sides from fighting.

NEGOTIATIONS
The UN tries to get the different sides in a war to talk about stopping the fighting and ending the war.

SANCTIONS
The UN persuades other countries to stop giving weapons to the sides which are fighting.

AID
The UN tries to help the people in the countries which are fighting by giving them food and shelter. These people are often forced to leave the country. They are called refugees.

ACTIVITIES

Copy out the heading:
How does the United Nations help to stop wars?

1 Copy out the 'What you will learn' box.

2 Copy and complete the following. Use the words given below:

The .... was set up in ...... by a number of countries in the world. It had 2 main purposes—to ...... war and to ...... countries which had problems such as not enough ....

Words
1945; food; help; stop; United Nations

THE UN IN ACTION
Play the Game on pages 38 and 39 and complete the activities below.

1   Here are some words from the game which you may not understand.
    Match the words with the correct definitions and write them in your jotter.

WORD
- ceasefire
- conflict
- convoy
- ethnic cleansing
- hostage
- observers
- refugees
- UN Security Council

DEFINITION
- fighting
- fighting stops
- people forced to flee from fighting
- groups of vehicles travelling together
- people who watch and report what is going on. They do not take part in the fighting.
- people held prisoner. They are set free if the other side meets some demands.
- a group of people being chased out or killed because they belong to a different group
- 15 countries which decide what the UN should do when there is a war

2   Find another word from the game which means the same as 'negotiations'.
3   "Aid convoy stopped by armed gangs."
    Why might an armed gang want to stop an aid convoy?
4   Describe two types of "bad weather" which might stop an aid convoy.
5   From the game, find and describe three ways in which a war can affect civilians.

Write out the heading: **Problems the UN can face in a conflict situation**
6   Go round the board and list as many problems as you can which the UN can face in a conflict situation.

Write out the heading: **What actions can the UN take to stop a war?**
7   Give details of the four actions which the UN can take to stop war.

CONFLICT

Throw 1 - 2
UN gets involved
Move to any
UN Action Space
Throw 3 - 4
UN ignored by both sides
Move forward 1 space
Throw 5 - 6
UN discusses problem
Throw again

Air Strikes
kill 1,400 people.
Dig mass grave.

MISS 1 TURN

Problem discussed
in UN Security
Council

**MOVE TO ANY
UN ACTION
SQUARE**

††††††††††††††††††††††
†††††††††††††††††††††††
††† **Ethnic** †††
†† **Cleansing** ††
†† ††
†† **MOVE BACK** ††
††† **4 SPACES** †††
†††††††††††††††††††††††
†††††††††††††††††††††††

Aid gets
through
to starvi
people

Daily News HORROR STORY & PICTURES ... page 5

CIVILIANS MASSACRED

UN ACTION PEACEKEEPING

THROW 1 - 4
FAILS TO STOP WAR
END OF TURN

THROW 5 - 6
WAR STOPS
PUT TOKEN ON
PEACEKEEPING BOX

Christmas ceasefire negotiated

Both sides refuse to talk

MISS 1 TURN

UN ACTION BOXES

NEGOTIATIONS
The UN has experts who try to get the sides to talk to each other to sort out their problems.

AID
The UN sends food, medical supplies, fuel and shelter to help the victims of war.

SANCTIONS
The UN tells its members to stop selling guns and other goods to the sides which are fighting.

PEACEKEEPING
UN sends soldiers to try to keep the peace between the sides.

UN IN

CONFLICT

Throw 1 - 2
UN gets involved
Move to any
UN Action Space
Throw 3 - 4
UN ignored by both sides
Move forward 1 space
Throw 5 - 6
UN discusses problem
Throw again

ROAD BLOCKS

MOVE BACK 6 SPACES

Refugees flee to neighbouring country

UN ACTION SANCTIONS

THROW 1 - 4
SANCTIONS FAIL
END OF TURN
THROW 5 - 6
SANCTIONS WORK
PUT TOKEN ON
SANCTIONS BOX

Sanctions stop weapons getting through

MOVE FORWARD 1 SPACE

UN ACTION AID

THROW 1 - 4
AID IS STOPPED
END OF TURN

THROW 5 - 6
AID GETS THROUGH
PUT TOKEN ON AID BOX

UN Observers sent in.

UN troops held hostage

THROW 3 TO RELEASE HOSTAGES

CONFLICT

Throw 1 - 2
UN gets involved
Move to any
UN Action Space
Throw 3 - 4
UN ignored by both sides
Move forward 1 space
Throw 5 - 6
UN discusses problem
Throw again

ACTION

Bad weather.
Aid convoy stopped.

MISS 1 TURN

Visit from UN officials

RULES

1 Any number of players can play – even one.
2 Each player makes 5 tokens.
3 Place token on any of the 4 CONFLICT SQUARES.
4 Players move clockwise round the board.
5 Roll 1 dice. Highest throw starts.
6 Follow instructions on the board then pass dice to player on your left.
7 The game continues until one player has 1 token on each of the 4 UN Action Boxes.

UN ACTION NEGOTIATIONS

THROW 1 - 4
TALKS FAIL
END OF TURN

THROW 5 - 6
TALKS SUCCEED
PUT TOKEN ON NEGOTIATIONS BOX

Shelling destroys large town. Many dead.

Sides agree to negotiate

MOVE FORWARD 5 SPACES

FORWARD 1 SPACE

UN delivers medical supplies

Aid convoy stopped by armed gangs.

MISS 1 TURN

CONFLICT

Throw 1 - 2
UN gets involved
Move to any
UN Action Space
Throw 3 - 4
UN ignored by both sides
Move forward 1 space
Throw 5 - 6
UN discusses problem
Throw again

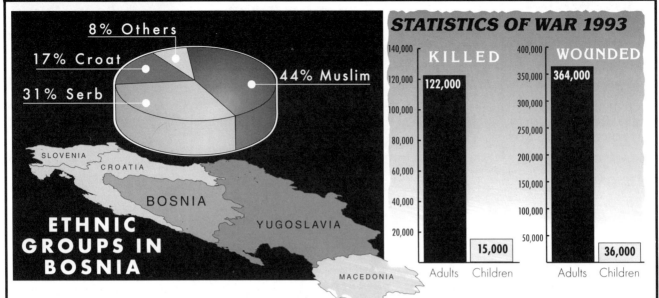

8% Others

17% Croat

31% Serb

44% Muslim

SLOVENIA

CROATIA

BOSNIA

YUGOSLAVIA

MACEDONIA

ETHNIC GROUPS IN BOSNIA

STATISTICS OF WAR 1993

KILLED — Adults 122,000, Children 15,000

WOUNDED — Adults 364,000, Children 36,000

WAR IN BOSNIA

- In 1991 Bosnia became independent from Yugoslavia.

- For many years the Muslims, Serbs and Croats have hated each other.

- Civil war broke out in Bosnia because Bosnian Serbs refused to be part of a country ruled by Bosnian Muslims. Croats refused to be part of Bosnia and wanted to be part of Croatia.

- Bosnian Serbs got weapons from Yugoslavia.

- Bosnian Serbs massacred Muslims or forced them to leave areas of Bosnia. This is called ethnic cleansing.

- 750,000 Muslim refugees were crowded into a few small areas of Bosnia.

UN ACTION IN BOSNIA

- The UN tried again and again to negotiate a ceasefire between all the sides to stop them fighting.

- The UN tried to get aid into parts of Bosnia to feed and clothe the victims of the civil war.

- The UN put sanctions on Yugoslavia to force it to stop sending weapons to the Bosnian Serbs.

- The UN sent peacekeeping forces to areas where peace had been negotiated. The UN peacekeepers watched what

REFUGEES CREATED BY THE WAR

1.8 million in Bosnia

1.8 million in other countries

each side was doing and tried to persuade them to stick to the agreements.

- The UN declared Bosnia to be a no-fly zone and certain areas to be safe havens. NATO shot down some planes and destroyed some guns until the Serbs and the Yugoslavs did what the UN wanted.

WAR IN BOSNIA

BIHAC
- Muslim area surrounded by Serb forces
- UN got aid through
- Aid cut off by Serbs

ZENICA
- No aid got through
- Food riots
- People starved

SRBRENICA
- UN peacekeepers in place
- Watched both sides to stop them killing each other

TRAVNIK
- Muslims killed by shelling
- UN tried to negotiate a ceasefire

SARAJEVO
- Shelled by Serb forces
- UN negotiated ceasefire between Muslims and Serbs
- Bosnian Serb snipers shot civilians including children and an 85-year-old woman
- UN convoys took aid into Sarajevo
- Bosnian Serbs stopped UN aid convoys from reaching Sarajevo

MOSTAR
- Muslim area surrounded by Serbs and Croats
- UN tried to negotiate ceasefire
- UN tried to deliver aid to help the refugees in Mostar

CROATIA

BOSNIA

SERBIA

Bihac

Srbrenica

Zenica

Travnik

Sarajevo

Mostar

MACEDONIA

ITALY

ALBANIA

Name of Paper   Adverts

UN HEADLINE

Main Story   Map

Story 3

Story 2

ACTIVITIES

Copy the heading: **The UN in Bosnia**

Read the information on pages 40 and 41 and complete the activities below.

1 Write down the names of the ethnic groups in Bosnia.

2 Draw a bar graph to show the percentage of the population in each ethnic group in Bosnia.

3 Why did the civil war start in Bosnia?

4 What has the UN done to try to stop the war in Bosnia?

5 What problems has the UN faced in trying to help the people of Bosnia?

6 You are going to write the front page of a newspaper.

On this page will be:

- The name of the newspaper.

- The main story which is about the UN and what it is trying to do in Bosnia. Give this story a headline.

- The second story will be about why the war started in Bosnia. Give this story a headline.

- The third story will be about statistics of the war in Bosnia. Give this story a headline.

- There will be a map of Bosnia and some of the things which have happened to the main towns. Give your map a title.

UNIT 6 – What is NATO?

What you will learn:

➤ NATO is a defence organisation

➤ Why NATO was needed

➤ That changes in Europe will affect NATO

Concepts: NEED and POWER

WHY WAS NATO NEEDED?

After the Second World War the USSR kept troops in the countries of Eastern Europe and set up communist governments in them. Germany was divided into two parts—capitalist West Germany and communist East Germany. Germany's capital city, Berlin, was divided into two—capitalist West Berlin and communist East Berlin. So many

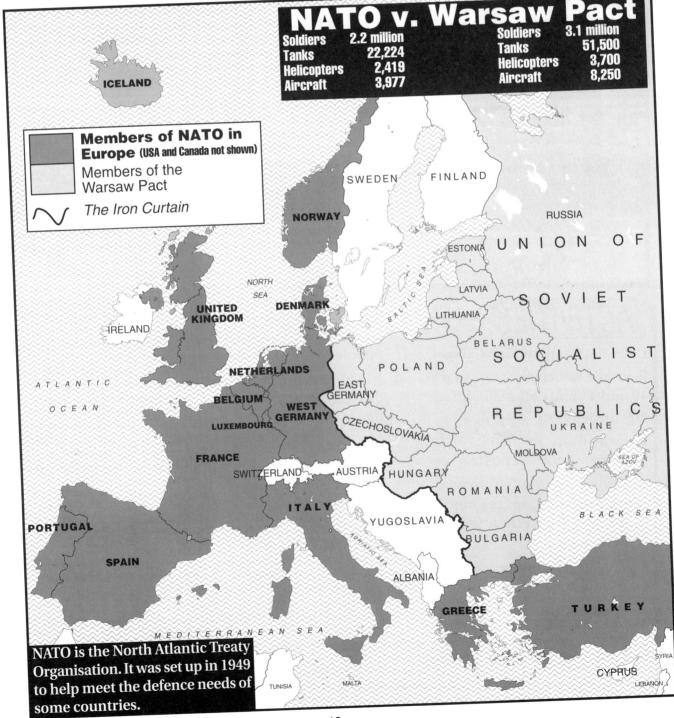

NATO v. Warsaw Pact			
Soldiers	2.2 million	Soldiers	3.1 million
Tanks	22,224	Tanks	51,500
Helicopters	2,419	Helicopters	3,700
Aircraft	3,977	Aircraft	8,250

Members of NATO in Europe (USA and Canada not shown)

Members of the Warsaw Pact

The Iron Curtain

NATO is the North Atlantic Treaty Organisation. It was set up in 1949 to help meet the defence needs of some countries.

people fled to West Berlin to escape communism that the Russians built a wall in 1961 to stop this.

In 1955 the Soviet Union set up a military organisation to help meet her defence needs. It was called the Warsaw Pact.

It was used to crush the people of Hungary in 1956 and the people of Czechoslovakia in 1968 when they tried to escape from the control of the Soviet Union.

THE NEWS—1961
BERLIN WALL BUILT

THE NEWS—1956
THE WARSAW PACT INVADES HUNGARY

THE NEWS—1968
WARSAW PACT INVADES CZECHOSLOVAKIA

THE NEWS—1945

NAZI GERMANY BEATEN
USSR occupies East Germany, Poland, Czechoslovakia, Hungary, Romania and Bulgaria.

THE NEWS—1949
NATO FORMED

The countries of Western Europe have agreed to join together to defend themselves. The Prime Minister said, "Each country by itself could not fight the USSR. Together we can."

THE NEWS—1955
WARSAW PACT FORMED

The communist countries in Eastern Europe have formed an alliance to defend themselves from NATO. These countries are: USSR, Poland, East Germany, Czechoslovakia, Hungary, Romania, Bulgaria and Albania.

ACTIVITIES

Copy the heading: **What is NATO and why was it needed?**

Copy the 'What you will learn box'.

Read the information on pages 42 and 43 and then do the activities which follow.

1 On a blank map of Europe, name and colour in the members of NATO in blue; name and colour in the Warsaw Pact countries in red.

2 The countries left are neutral. What does neutral mean? (Use a dictionary to help you.)

3 Here are some statements. Write down the ones which are true under the heading 'Why was NATO needed?'

● In 1945 the USA invaded Czechoslovakia, East Germany, Hungary and Poland.

● In 1945 the USSR invaded Czechoslovakia, East Germany, Hungary and Poland.

■ NATO was formed by the communist countries in Eastern Europe in 1949.

■ NATO was formed by countries in Western Europe to defend themselves against the communist countries in Eastern Europe.

▲ In 1955 the communist countries in Eastern Europe formed the Warsaw Pact to defend themselves from NATO.

▲ In 1955 the communist countries in Western Europe formed NATO to defend themselves from the Warsaw Pact.

✳ The threat from the Warsaw Pact was shown in 1956 when it invaded Hungary and again in 1968 when it invaded Czechoslovakia.

✳ The threat from NATO was shown in 1956 when it invaded Hungary and again in 1968 when it invaded Czechoslovakia.

4 Give two reasons to explain why NATO was needed.

ALL CHANGE IN EUROPE

In 1985, Mikhail Gorbachev, became the leader of the USSR. He promised to make changes and to allow people to have more freedom.

By 1992 the USSR had broken up into fifteen different countries. Communism had collapsed in Eastern Europe. New countries were created. Some are shown on the map opposite. The Warsaw Pact no longer existed.

ACTIVITIES

Copy the heading:

All change in Europe

Read all the information on All Change in Europe.

1 You are a reporter reporting on the situation in Europe. Your job is to make up the front page of a newspaper with the following bits of information on it:

● Headline:
All change in Europe

● Map of Europe before 1989

● Map of Europe today

● Reasons for the changes in Europe

Right: The Berlin Wall was overrun by people from East and West Berlin in 1990

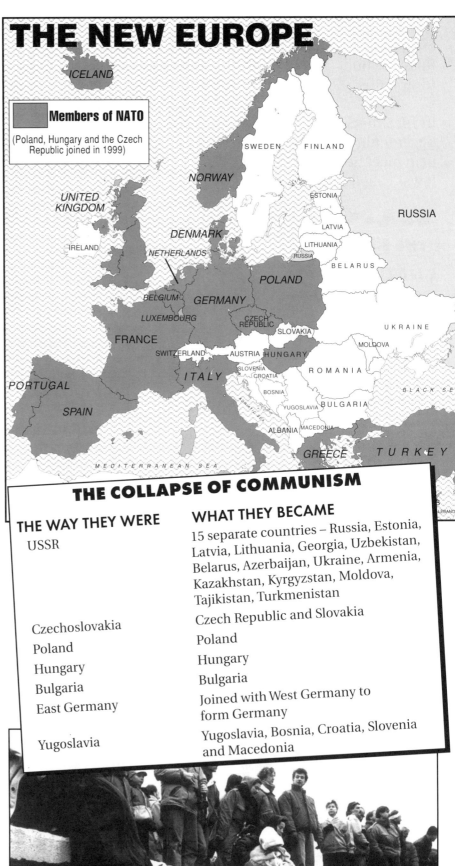

THE NEW EUROPE

Members of NATO

(Poland, Hungary and the Czech Republic joined in 1999)

THE COLLAPSE OF COMMUNISM

THE WAY THEY WERE	WHAT THEY BECAME
USSR	15 separate countries – Russia, Estonia, Latvia, Lithuania, Georgia, Uzbekistan, Belarus, Azerbaijan, Ukraine, Armenia, Kazakhstan, Kyrgyzstan, Moldova, Tajikistan, Turkmenistan
Czechoslovakia	Czech Republic and Slovakia
Poland	Poland
Hungary	Hungary
Bulgaria	Bulgaria
East Germany	Joined with West Germany to form Germany
Yugoslavia	Yugoslavia, Bosnia, Croatia, Slovenia and Macedonia

Enquiry Skills

INVESTIGATING USING A VIDEO

You are investigating how Europe changed in 1989. You are going to use a video to gather information. To use a video effectively you should:

- know before you watch the video what information you are looking for.
- use bullet points or a spider diagram to organise your notes.
- write up your notes as soon as possible.

Using a video to investigate something has some good points and some bad points.

Good points

- you can watch it again and again.
- the pictures help to explain what is being said.
- you can see things you would not see otherwise.
- most people have access to video recorders at school and at home.

Bad points

- videos might not give an accurate account of what happened. You only see it from one point of view.
- videos might be too complicated, using difficult ideas and language.
- the programme could be out of date.
- video tape deteriorates and you cannot get a good picture as it gets older.

NATO – MEETING THE DEFENCE NEEDS OF EUROPE

NATO meets the defence and military needs of Europe in the following ways.

- The members organise and plan their military forces in a cooperative way.
- The members share the costs of equipment such as weapons.
- The members have a Collective Defence Policy. This means that if any member is attacked this would be seen as an attack on all of the members of NATO. The country under attack would be supported by NATO members.

ACTIVITIES

Copy the heading: **Nato-meeting the defence needs of Europe**

1 Dewscribe two ways in which Nato helps to meet the defence needs of Europe.

2 Explain what 'Collective defence policy' means.

ACTIVITIES

Copy the heading: **Enquiry Skills - Investigating using video**

1 What do you have to do to use a video effectively?

2 Copy the statements below about using videos. Beside each statement write down whether it is a good point or a bad point.

- you can watch it again and again.
- the pictures help to explain what is being said.
- videos might be too complicated, using difficult ideas and language.
- videos might not give an accurate account of what happened. You only see it from one point of view.
- you can see things you would not see otherwise.
- video tape deteriorates and you cannot get a good picture as it gets older.
- the programme could be out of date.
- most people have access to video recorders at school and at home.

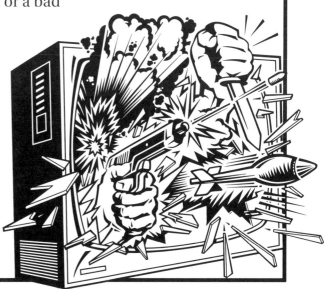

IS NATO STILL NEEDED?

We should scrap NATO because the Warsaw Pact does not exist any more.

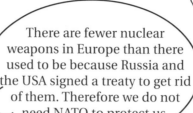
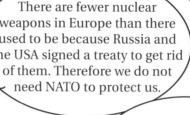

We do not need NATO because the USSR has broken up into smaller countries. It does not threaten us any more.

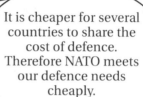

There are fewer nuclear weapons in Europe than there used to be because Russia and the USA signed a treaty to get rid of them. Therefore we do not need NATO to protect us.

It is cheaper for several countries to share the cost of defence. Therefore NATO meets our defence needs cheaply.

If countries co-operate with each other in a defence alliance other countries are less likely to attack them. So we still need NATO.

Instead of spending money on weapons for NATO we could build more hospitals, schools and roads. That would mean better services and more jobs for people in this country. We would be better off without NATO.

We need to keep NATO. There are more states in Eastern Europe with nuclear weapons. They could threaten us.

There has been war between Russia and other states in the East. There has been war in Bosnia. If some country launched its nuclear weapons we could all get involved. We need NATO to carry on protecting us.

ACTIVITIES

Study the information above. There are eight statements. Four statements support keeping NATO and four statements are against keeping NATO.

1 Copy and complete the table below by putting the statements under the correct heading in the table.

ARGUMENTS FOR KEEPING **NATO**	ARGUMENTS AGAINST KEEPING **NATO**

2 Use the information in the table you have completed.

   "We must continue in NATO to meet our defence needs in the new millenium."

   Do you agree or disagree with this statement? Give two reasons to support your point of view.

ARMS AGREEMENTS

From the end of the Second World War, the USA and the USSR were involved in a race to build more and more and bigger and better weapons.

By the end of the 1980s, both sides had enough nuclear weapons to kill every living person on Earth at least 30 times over. This competition was known as the Arms Race.

However, both sides realised that this was very dangerous. They could destroy all life on the planet. They eventually began to talk about stopping the arms race and reducing the number of weapons which they both possessed.

Factfile: Arms Agreements

1963 Partial Test Ban Treaty

The USA, the USSR and the UK agreed to stop testing nuclear weapons in the atmosphere. France continued to do so.

1968 Nuclear Non-Proliferation Treaty

This treaty was designed to stop the spread of the knowledge and the technology required to make nuclear weapons. In theory each country with nuclear weapons must have developed them by themselves, with their own expertise and raw materials.

1972 Strategic Arms Limitation Treaty (SALT 1)

This treaty set upper limits for how many long-range nuclear missiles each country could have.

1979 SALT 2

SALT 2 extended the previous talks and set new limits for strategic nuclear missiles.

1987 INF Treaty (Intermediate Nuclear Forces)

This treaty dealt with short- and medium-range nuclear missiles—the type which could be used in Europe. All land-based weapons in these categories were to be destroyed within three years. The USA and the USSR had access to each other's sites for verification of the treaty.

The INF Treaty did not include submarine-launched missiles.

1990 Conventional Forces in Europe Treaty (CFE)

The Warsaw Pact countries always had a huge advantage in terms of numbers of conventional weapons. This treaty evened out the mili-

tary balance in Europe, setting maximum numbers for tanks, artillery, armoured vehicles etc.

1991 Strategic Arms Reduction Treaty (START 1)

Around 30% of the really destructive Intercontinental Ballistic Missiles were destroyed. These are the type of missiles which could be launched from the USA and wipe out Moscow within an hour. There will be a maximum of 6,000 nuclear warheads by the year 2000, each still capable of killing hundreds of thousands of people.

1993 START 2

This treaty built on the progress made in START 1. All Intercontinental Ballistic Missiles are to be eliminated from the year 2003. Only submarine-launched and mobile warheads will remain. The total number of nuclear warheads will be reduced from 6,000 to about 3,500.

ACTIVITIES

Copy the heading:

Arms agreements

1 What was the arms race?

2 Make up a timeline to show the main arms agreements from 1963 to 1993.

You should put on it the name of each arms agreement. You should write a short paragraph about each arms agreement.

You may illustrate your timeline with drawings of weapons taken from the information.

UNIT 7 – Providing the economic needs of countries in Europe

What you will learn:

➤ That countries have economic needs

➤ That the needs of countries are met through cooperation

Concepts: NEED and POWER

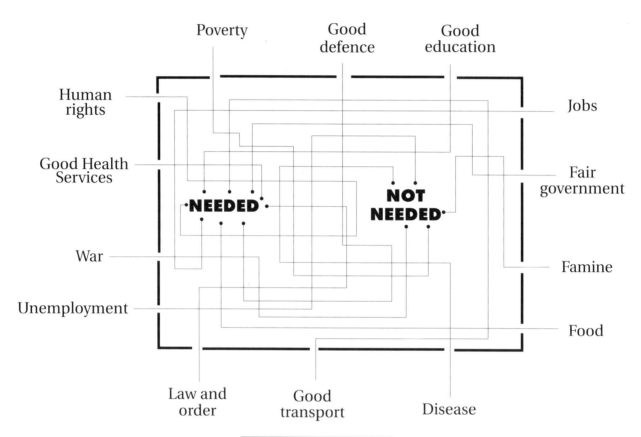

THE NEEDS OF COUNTRIES

Like people, countries have needs. People need, for example, food, water, shelter, health care, education, jobs, leisure time and protection from crime. People live in countries so the needs of countries are similar. In this section, we will concentrate on economic needs of countries such as getting enough food to feed their people and having enough jobs to give people a reasonable standard of living.

ACTIVITIES

Copy the heading: **The needs of countries**

Copy out the 'What you will learn' box.

1 Copy and complete this table. Put the words which are around the maze under the correct heading.

WHAT A COUNTRY NEEDS	WHAT A COUNTRY DOES NOT NEED

2 Mike Kane says, "The main needs of a country are food, poverty and disease."

Using the information in your table, is this statement true or not true?

Give a reason for your answer.

THE NEWS 1945

WAR ENDS
Europe in Ruins

World War Two has ended. Europe has been destroyed by the war. Factories have been bombed so they cannot produce things for people to buy. No one can work in these factories so there are no **jobs**. People have no wages so they have a **low** standard of living.

Many people have been killed in the war. Many more are starving because there is not enough food. Farmland has been destroyed by the armies fighting over it. There is no **food**.

Roads, railways and bridges have been blown up. Therefore it is difficult for countries to trade with each other.

The people need houses, food, jobs and the transport system needs to be re-built. The countries of Europe must co-operate if these needs are to be met.

THE NEWS 1957

EUROPEAN UNION SET UP
Countries cooperate for a better future

Six countries in Europe have agreed to cooperate with each other to help meet their economic needs. They will cooperate with each other to exchange the goods they produce. They will help each other to build new factories. This will mean more **jobs**. **Roads** will be improved. This means that countries can trade with each other. The European Union will also help farmers to grow more **food** to feed the people. Cooperation will give the people a **high** standard of living.

ACTIVITIES

Copy the heading: **Economic needs are met through cooperation**

1 Copy the *conflict flow chart* diagram.

Fill in the missing words using the information on this page.
The words you need are highlighted in the newspapers.

2 Copy the *cooperation flow chart* diagram.

Fill in the missing words using the information on this page.
The words you need are highlighted in the newspapers.

CONFLICT FLOW CHART

Conflict
|
World War Two
|
Europe is destroyed by war

farmland destroyed	factories bombed	----- destroyed
no -----	no -----	no trade with other countries

----- standard of living

COOPERATION FLOW CHART

Cooperation
|
European Union set up
|
Countries cooperate in a number of ways

improve farms	build factories	build -----
more -----	more -----	more trade

----- standard of living

THE EUROPEAN UNION TODAY

KEY
- ▲ Capital city
- ⊕ Money
- 👥 Population
- ◎ Food /drink
- ✹ Date joined EU

SWEDEN
- ▲ Stockholm
- ⊕ Krona
- 👥 8.8 million
- ◎ Smorgasborg
- ✹ 1995

FINLAND
- ▲ Helsinki
- ⊕ Markka
- 👥 5 million
- ◎ Reindeer stew
- ✹ 1995

BELGIUM
- ▲ Brussels
- ⊕ Franc
- 👥 10 million
- ◎ Chocolate
- ✹ 1957

UNITED KINGDOM
- ▲ London
- ⊕ Pound
- 👥 57.6 million
- ◎ Fish & Chips
- ✹ 1973

DENMARK
- ▲ Copenhagen
- ⊕ Kroner
- 👥 5.1 million
- ◎ Bacon
- ✹ 1973

LUXEMBOURG
- ▲ Luxembourg
- ⊕ Franc
- 👥 0.4 million
- ◎ Beer
- ✹ 1957

IRELAND
- ▲ Dublin
- ⊕ Punt
- 👥 3.5 million
- ◎ Guinness
- ✹ 1973

GERMANY
- ▲ Berlin
- ⊕ Mark
- 👥 79 million
- ◎ Sauerkraut
- ✹ 1957

NETHERLANDS
- ▲ The Hague
- ⊕ Guilder
- 👥 15 million
- ◎ Edam cheese
- ✹ 1957

AUSTRIA
- ▲ Vienna
- ⊕ Schilling
- 👥 7.7 million
- ◎ Schnitzel
- ✹ 1995

ITALY
- ▲ Rome
- ⊕ Lire
- 👥 58 million
- ◎ Spaghetti
- ✹ 1957

PORTUGAL
- ▲ Lisbon
- ⊕ Escudo
- 👥 10.5 million
- ◎ Sardines
- ✹ 1986

SPAIN
- ▲ Madrid
- ⊕ Peseta
- 👥 39 million
- ◎ Paella
- ✹ 1986

FRANCE
- ▲ Paris
- ⊕ Franc
- 👥 56 million
- ◎ Wine
- ✹ 1957

GREECE
- ▲ Athens
- ⊕ Drachma
- 👥 10 million
- ◎ Hummus
- ✹ 1981

◪ ACTIVITIES

Get a blank map of Europe from your teacher.

1 Give your map a heading: **The Countries in the European Union**.

2 Name the 15 countries in the EU.

3 Colour in the countries as follows
   Countries which joined the EU in 1957 – *red*
   Countries which joined the EU in 1973 – *blue*
   Countries which joined the EU in 1981 – *yellow*
   Countries which joined the EU in 1986 – *green*
   Countries which joined the EU in 1995 – *orange*

4 Give your map a key to show what each colour means—eg. *yellow – joined in 1981*.

5 Copy and complete the word tree using the information from the map on page 50.

__ T __	
__ H _____	- Its currency is the Guilder.
__ E ____	- Its population is 8.8 million.
__ E __	- Guinness is its favourite drink.
__ U _____	- The capital is Vienna.
__ R ____	- Joined the European Union in 1981.
_____ O _	- Fish and chips are its favourite food.
__ P ___	- 320 pesetas for paella.
__ E ____	- Between France and the Netherlands
__ A _____	- Rome is its capital.
_____ N _	- The largest population in the EU.
_____ U ____	- The smallest population in the EU.
__ N __	- Vin, s'il vous plait? You're under age!
__ I ____	- Markka is the currency.
__ O _____	- Sardines on toast a speciality.
__ N __	- Copenhagen is the capital.

EU MEETING NEEDS – FOOD

Brian got up one Sunday morning. He is a big lad and his mum likes to feed him well. For his breakfast she gave him orange juice, cornflakes with milk and sugar, bacon, egg, sausage, fried tomato, fried mushrooms, toast and butter and a cup of tea.

The tea came from India. The corn-flakes came from the USA. All the rest of the food was produced in countries which are in the European Union.

Breakfast from Europe

SWEDEN · FINLAND · UNITED KINGDOM · IRELAND · DENMARK · NETHERLANDS · GERMANY · BELGIUM · LUX · FRANCE · AUSTRIA · ITALY · PORTUGAL · SPAIN · GREECE

SUGAR from *Germany*

IRISH BUTTER

TASTE OF EU SURVEY

Brian surveyed 20 people to find out how many had tried foods from different countries in the EU. Here is the result of his survey.

FOOD	Tried & liked	Tried & disliked	Never tried
Pizza	卌 卌 卌 II	III	IIII
Spaghetti	卌 卌	卌 I	卌 I
Haggis	卌 IIII	卌	卌 卌 II
Croissants	卌	III	II
Sardines	卌 卌 III	III	卌 卌 II
Paella	卌	III	卌 卌 I
Kebabs	卌	IIII	卌 卌 卌 卌
Paté			
Fish and Chips	卌 卌 卌 IIII	I	

ACTIVITIES

Copy the heading: **European Union Meeting Needs – Food**

1 Complete the following paragraph.

   Brian depends on the European Union for his breakfast. Brian had sausages, eggs and milk which came from the UK. The mushrooms he ate came from ......

   Continue the paragraph until you have mentioned everything Brian had for breakfast and which countries in the EU it all came from.

2 You are going to write a report about what Brian found out in his food survey.

   Here is a report which needs some information to complete it. Use Brian's findings to complete the report.

   REPORT ON … (*complete to make an appropriate heading*)

   Introduction

   I wanted to find out how many people ate food from countries in the European Union. I surveyed _ _ people to find out how many of them had tried different types of _ _ _ _ from countries in the EU. This is what I found out.

   Pizza

   Pizza is a food which comes from Italy. As the graph shows, 17 people had tried and liked pizza and only 3 did not like it. Everyone I asked had tried pizza.

   Spaghetti

   Spaghetti is a food which comes from Italy. As the graph shows, 10 people had tried and liked spaghetti. Only 6 did not like it. 4 people had never tried spaghetti.

   Haggis

   Haggis is a food which comes from Scotland. As the graph shows, _ people had tried and liked haggis. Only _ did not like it. _ people had never tried haggis.

Draw a graph to show these results.
Complete this report for the rest of the foods in the survey.

   Conclusion

   I found out that the most popular food was fish and chips, which comes from Britain, followed by pizza which comes from Italy. Most people had not tried paella, croissants and kebabs. Nobody had tried paté. We eat some foods from EU countries but there are foods which many people have not tried.

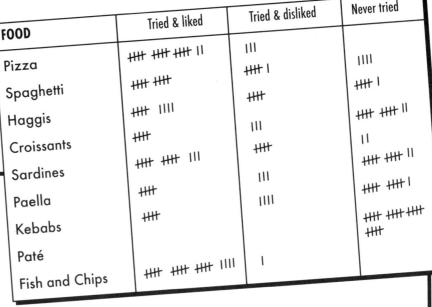

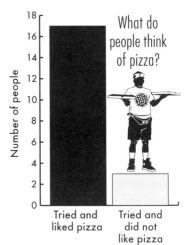

What do people think of pizza?

Number of people

Tried and liked pizza / Tried and did not like pizza

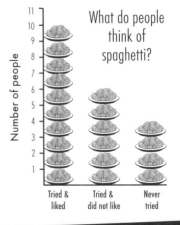

What do people think of spaghetti?

Number of people

Tried & liked / Tried & did not like / Never tried

Try this survey for yourself and write up your own report. Here are some hints.
- Survey at least 20 people
- Record the results using tally marks
- Turn your results into graphs
- Write up your report using the example above to help you
- Remember, all reports must have an Introduction and a Conclusion.

Enquiry Skills

INVESTIGATING USING QUESTIONNAIRES AND SURVEYS

A questionnaire or a survey is a list of questions which you want answered. The answers should give you information about the topic you are investigating.

A questionnaire should have open questions which try to get more detailed information from the people answering them. A questionnaire is usually restricted to a small sample (the number of people being questioned).

A survey usually has closed questions which allow people to give a one-word answer or to choose one item from a list. A survey is usually for a large sample of people.

WHAT ARE OPEN QUESTIONS AND CLOSED QUESTIONS?
An open question allows the person to give a long answer or explanation. Here are some examples of open questions.
- What are your views on Britain being part of the European Union?
- What do you think are the advantages of Britain being part of the European Union?

A closed question allows the person to say 'yes' or 'no' or give a very short answer which does not give you any detailed information about the topic. Here are some examples of closed questions.
- Should Britain be part of the European Union?
- Are there any advantages to Britain being part of the European Union?

GOOD POINTS
- The questions cover the topic you are investigating exactly.
- You can ask only people you want.
- You can get fast results.

BAD POINTS
- People might not want to answer your questions.
- People might not understand your questions.
- You might get too much or too little information and this may make it difficult to interpret your survey.

ACTIVITIES

Copy the heading: **Enquiry Skills – Investigating using Questionnaires and Surveys**

1 What is a survey?
2 What is a questionnaire?
3 When would it be better to use a survey rather than a questionnaire? Give a reason for your answer.
4 What is an open question?
5 What is a closed question?
6 Make up two open questions of your own about the European Union.
7 Make up two closed questions of your own about the European Union.
9 Why is using a survey a good way to investigate people's opinions about the European Union?
10 Copy the statements below about using questionnaires and surveys. Beside each statement write down whether it is a good point or a bad point.
- People might not understand your questions.
- The questions cover the topic you are investigating exactly.
- People might not want to answer your questions.
- You can get fast results.
- You might get too much or too little information and this may make it difficult to interpret your survey.
- You can ask only people you want.

UNIT 8 – Cooperation in the European Union

┌─ What you will learn: ─────────────────────────┐
➤ That the needs of countries are met through cooperation
└──┘

Concepts: NEED and POWER

THE COMMON AGRICULTURAL POLICY

In the EU, countries are meant to co-operate with each other to make sure there is enough food for everyone. They do this through the Common Agricultural Policy (CAP).

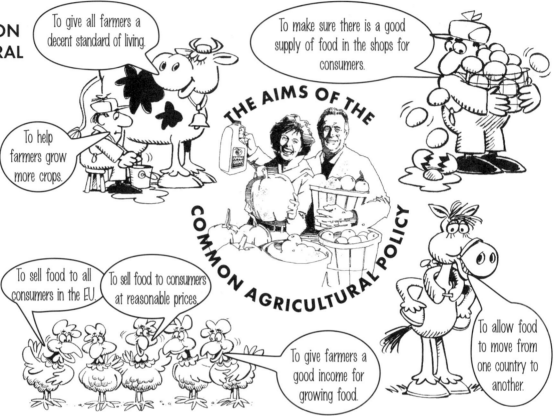

THE AIMS OF THE COMMON AGRICULTURAL POLICY

To give all farmers a decent standard of living.

To make sure there is a good supply of food in the shops for consumers.

To help farmers grow more crops.

To sell food to all consumers in the EU.

To sell food to consumers at reasonable prices.

To give farmers a good income for growing food.

To allow food to move from one country to another.

ACTIVITIES

Copy the heading: **Cooperation in the EU – the Common Agricultural Policy**

1 Copy out the Aims of the Common Agricultural Policy.

2

View A
I do not think the CAP is any good. It does nothing to help farmers.

View B
I think the CAP is good because it helps farmers.

Using the information on this page, which view do you agree with? Give two reasons to support your point of view.

3

View A
The CAP does nothing to help consumers in the EU.

View B
The CAP helps consumers in the EU.

Using the information on this page, which view do you agree with? Give two reasons to support your point of view.

LAMBS TO THE SLAUGHTER

Yesterday the streets of Bellac in France were littered with the bodies of 300 British lambs which had been killed by French farmers. They hijacked a lorry which was carrying lambs on their way to a slaughterhouse. They killed the lambs and the carcasses were left to rot in the streets so that they could not be sold.

The French farmers are protesting at the import of lamb from Britain and other countries in the EU. These countries can sell lamb more cheaply than the French can sell their lamb. The French farmers claim that government subsidies to British farmers are more than the subsidies they get in France. 75% of British lamb is sold to France.

The French farmers want their government to stop the import of cheap British lamb into France. One French farmer said, "cheap imports mean that I can't sell my lamb so my standard of living gets worse".

French farmers have used many types of violence
* blocking motorways with tractors
* dumping tons of manure across roads
* hijacking and burning lorries
* throwing bottles
* attacking the police
* beating up drivers

55

ACTIVITIES

1 Reorganise these sentences to make up a newspaper article about the lamb wars. Put the sentences into paragraphs. Give your article a title.

- British lorries have been stopped and set on fire by French farmers.

- British lamb is cheaper than French lamb.

- French farmers do not like British lamb coming into France.

- French farmers say that British lamb is cheaper because British lamb is subsidised.

- French farmers have protested by blocking roads with manure and by hijacking lorries and killing the lambs.

- French farmers cannot sell their lamb so they are poorer.

- The French farmers want the government to stop imports of cheap British lamb into France.

2 Imagine you are the television reporter. You have to sum up at the end of the interviews. You must put into your own words the main points made by Jacques Agneau, Fred Shepherd and Marie Shellac.

COOPERATION IN THE EU – THE EUROCAR

Most cars are put together from parts which are made in a number of countries. Most of the cars we see are assembled from parts made in a number of EU countries. Opposite is an example of one car and the countries in which the parts are made.

Cooperation among EU countries is important because people's jobs and living standards depend on it.

CAR PART	COUNTRY WHERE IT IS MADE
Body	UK
Windscreen	Austria
Engine	Germany
Windscreen wipers	Luxembourg
Lights	Italy
Tyres	France
Exhaust	Belgium
Wheels	Ireland

ACTIVITIES

Copy the heading:
Cooperation in the EU – The EuroCar

1 Copy a diagram of a car.

2 Label your drawing to show where the different parts come from.

3 The car is assembled in the UK. What would happen to the workers in the UK if the workers who make the engines in Germany went on strike?

  (Think about the number of cars which can be made and the effect on British wages.)

4 In what way do car workers in the UK depend on car workers in other countries in the EU?

5 Car Park Survey:

  • You are going to carry out a survey of cars in the school car park.

  • Look for these models of car – Saab (Sweden); BMW, Volkswagen, Mercedes, Audi (Germany); Fiat (Italy); Renault, Peugeot, Citroën (France); Seat (Spain); British cars.

  • To help you to carry out the survey look back at page 52.

COOPERATION IN THE EU – THE EUROFIGHTER

WHAT IS THE EUROFIGHTER TYPHOON?

The Eurofighter Typhoon is the most advanced fighter aircraft being designed for the 21st century. It is being developed by four European countries cooperating with one another—United Kingdom, Germany, Italy and Spain. The plane can fly at speeds of over 15,000mph—faster than a speeding bullet—and can travel at more than twice the speed of sound. It could fly from London to Paris in 8 minutes! The pilot's helmet system allows him to direct and fire a missile just by looking at the target. Over 6.5 tonnes of weapons can be carried—twice the amount carried by a World War Two bomber such as the British Lancaster.

Modern technology means that the Eurofighter Typhoon can be made in 18 months. It normally takes 4 years to build a fighter aircraft.

WHAT COOPERATION IS TAKING PLACE?

It is being developed by four countries cooperating with each other—United Kingdom, Germany, Italy and Spain.

The companies involved are:
+ British Aerospace
+ Germany's Daimler Benz Aerospace
+ Alenia Aerospazio of Italy
+ CASA of Spain

The project is being coordinated through the Eurofighter headquarters in Munich, Germany.

WHAT ARE THE BENEFITS OF COOPERATION?

✔ The countries involved are less likely to start fighting each other so there is less chance of war.

✔ Europe's aerospace industry becomes the best in the world. This helps trade.

✔ All the countries involved save money because they can share the costs and share their expertise.

✔ Jobs are created. 150,000 high technology jobs will be created within 400 companies for at least the next 20 years.

ACTIVITIES

Copy the heading:
Cooperation in the EU – the Eurofighter

1 Make up a leaflet about the Eurofighter. Use these headings to help you.
  • WHAT IS THE EUROFIGHTER?
  • WHY IS IT SUCH AN ADVANCED PLANE?
  • WHAT COOPERATION IS TAKING PLACE?
  • WHAT ARE THE BENEFITS OF COOPERATION?

2 Do you think that cooperation like this is good? Give two reasons for your answer.

ACTIVITIES

Copy the heading :
Cooperation in the EU – Aid to the regions

Use the information on page 58.

1 Why does Scotland get help from the European Union?

2 Why does the EU give money to the regions?

3 When the EU gives money to a project, which other sources must already have given funding?

4 Give some examples of projects funded by the EU and the amount of money they have given.

Aid to the Regions

EU Factfile: *Why help the Regions?* (1)

Scotland gets financial help from the European Union because it is a poor region compared to other areas. There are five reasons why the EU gives money to the regions.

1. To help regions which are not developing fast enough.
2. To help areas which have suffered from serious industrial decline.
3. To try to tackle long-term unemployment.
4. To provide work for young people.
5. To develop rural areas.

EU Factfile: *Why help the Regions?* (2)

The Highlands and Islands of Scotland get money from the EU because the average income of people in the region is only 75% of the average in the EU.

Much of Central Scotland gets help from the EU because industries like coal mining, iron and steel, and shipbuilding as well as other manufacturing industries have closed down over the past thirty years.

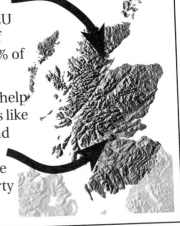

EU Factfile: *EU Money* (1)

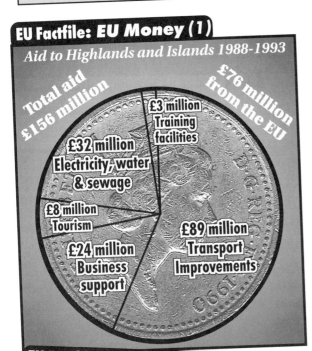

Aid to Highlands and Islands 1988-1993

Total aid £156 million — £76 million from the EU

- £3 million Training facilities
- £32 million Electricity, water & sewage
- £8 million Tourism
- £24 million Business support
- £89 million Transport Improvements

EU Factfile: *EU Projects*

Examples of Projects funded by EU Aid

- £ Ferry services to the Western Isles.
- £ Causeway from Barra to Watersay.
- £ Improvements to Inverness airport.
- £ Improvements to Tiree airstrip.
- £ Electrification of Glasgow – Largs railway.
- £ Heightening the Carron dam to create a larger reservoir to provide more water for people in Central Scotland.
- £ Dundee sewer project.
- £ New bird observatory on Fair Isle.
- £ Pedestrianisation of Alloa town centre.
- £ New industrial/business park and retail development at Stirling.

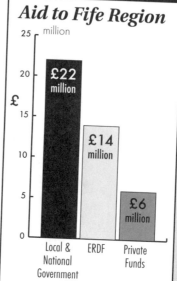

EU Factfile: *EU Money* (2)

The main source of funds for Scotland is the European Regional Development Fund (ERDF).

The EU gives money on three conditions.

1. The national government and the local government must be involved in the project before the EU will be involved.
2. The control of the project must be at local level.
3. The money given by the EU must be in addition to money already given to the project from sources in the country. EU money must not replace any funds already set aside for the project.

EU Factfile: *Aid to Fife*

Aid to Fife Region

million / £

- £22 million — Local & National Government
- £14 million — ERDF
- £6 million — Private Funds

Projects

- units for small businesses at Kirkcaldy
- improvements to the road and rail network
- improvements to Cowdenbeath and Glenrothes town centres
- tourist developments such as the Fife Coastal Footpath

Paris, France
27 June

Dear Lisa,

Everything is great here in Paris. I was really lucky. I got a job as an entertainer in Eurodisney. Some days I'm Mickey Mouse and other days I'm a cowboy at the OK Corral. Never a dull moment.

You should think about getting a job in France. Maybe even here in Eurodisney Paris. I suppose you are still unemployed. There are so few well-paid jobs in Scotland. I know my job is only temporary but the pay is quite good. I've rented a nice flat and have enough money to enjoy myself. You do not really need any experience but it does help to speak a bit of French.

I'm trying to get a job as a computer operator. My qualifications are recognised here—in fact they are recognised in every country in the EU. I also qualify for benefits from the French social security. In September I am going to college in Paris to get extra qualifications. Then I will try for a job somewhere else in the EU.

It is not too difficult to get a job in Europe. If you are interested check with the Job Centre in the town. They will put you on to the Job Club. They will give you information about residential permits etc. Start looking in newspapers. There is usually a list of jobs abroad. That's how I got my Disney job.

Must go. I'm Mickey Mouse today. Maybe see you in Paris before too long.

love
Wendy

ACTIVITIES

Copy the heading: **Cooperation in the EU – Movement of Workers**

Read Wendy's letter and answer the following questions in sentences.

1 Where is Wendy working?
2 Why did Wendy leave Scotland to get a job in France?
3 What does she enjoy about her job?
4 What might life be like for Wendy if she had stayed in Scotland?
5 Wendy can apply for a job as a computer operator in any country in the EU. Why is this possible?
6 If Wendy became unemployed in France would she be entitled to claim benefits?
7 What can Lisa do to find a job in Europe?

ACTIVITIES

Read Lisa's letter and answer the following questions in sentences.

1 Juergen has been in Scotland twice. Why was he here? Give two reasons.
2 What do you think Lisa means when she says that Europe is "one big country, not fifteen separate countries"?
3 People can get a job in any country in the European Union. In what ways can the needs of a country be met by the free movement of workers?

Dear Wendy,

Life sounds great in Paris. I'm thinking seriously about getting a job somewhere in the EU. I met a guy in a disco last week. His name is Juergen. He is blond and so good looking. He comes from Munich in Germany. He is here in Scotland for a year doing a college course.

He wants to work in Scotland when he is finished college because he likes walking in the Scottish mountains.

When he was at school he did two weeks work experience in Glasgow in a bank. When we were at school some of the 4th year went on a work experience to Denmark. Remember Sally said she worked in a nursery school? She said it was a great experience.

It seems like Europe is part of the UK. I guess that's how it's meant to be—one big country, not fifteen separate countries.

Juergen says that it is easy to get a job as a barmaid in one of the beer gardens in Munich. Maybe I'll try there. Maybe I should go to evening classes to learn German.

lots of love
Lisa

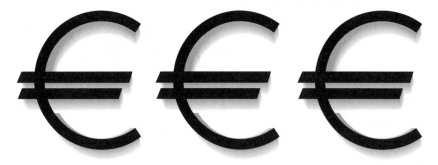

Survey of UK Citizens
about joining the euro

The Secretariat
The European Union
Strasburg
15 February 1999

Dear Lindsey,

Thank you for your letter asking about the euro. I hope the answers help you with your investigation.

1 What is the euro?
The euro is a new currency for countries which are members of the European Union. The European Central Bank is in charge of controlling the euro.

2 When was the euro introduced?
It was introduced on 1 January, 1999. Between 1999 and 2002 electronic money transactions in euros can be made between countries. However, notes and coins will not be issued until 1 January, 2002. Therefore people will not have euros in their wallets or purses until 2002.

3 Have all members of the European Union joined?
No.

4 I have read about the Euroland. Please explain what this means.
The Euroland is the name given to the countries which decided to issue the euro. Eleven countries out of the 15 EU members are in the Euroland. The 4 countries which did not join were the UK, Sweden, Denmark and Greece. Greece wanted to join but its economy was not strong enough. The others opted not to take part.

5 If I go on holiday to a country in the Euroland, what differences will it make to me?
If you use cash, you will still have to buy goods in the local currency. However, if you use traveller's cheques you will get Eurocheques. Unlike normal traveller's cheques you will not have to pay commission on a Eurocheque.

Yours sincerely,

Frank Kroner

Do you think that it is inevitable that Britain will join the euro?

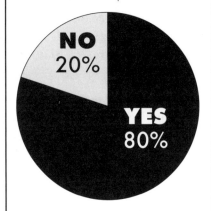

Do you think the UK should have joined the euro in 1999?

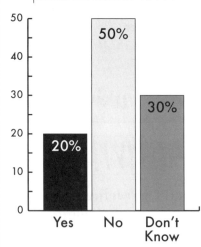

The UK government is waiting to see if it wants to join the euro. Do you support this?

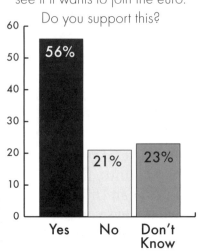

REASONS FOR JOINING THE EURO

- You can travel to any country in Euroland and use the same money.
- You do not have to work out exchange rates when buying something abroad.
- A car which costs 12,000 euros in the UK is far more expensive than the same car costing 9,000 euros in France.
- It encourages competition so prices should fall.
- Britain can join with other Euroland countries to fix interest rates. We would have a say in what happened with the euro.

REASONS FOR NOT JOINING THE EURO

- We will keep control over our economy.
- The Queen's head would no longer be on our currency.
- Getting 15 countries to co-operate is difficult and could lead to high unemployment.
- It would eventually lead to a 'United States of Europe' and we would no longer have a Parliament in Britain.
- It would give us a chance to wait and see if it is a success or a failure.

EUROLAND

Members of the EU which joined the euro in 1999

Members of the EU which did not join the euro in 1999

ACTIVITIES

1 Read pages 60 and 61. The information has been sent to you for an investigation you are doing on the euro. You are going to use all of the information to complete a wall poster about the euro. A model for your poster is shown below.

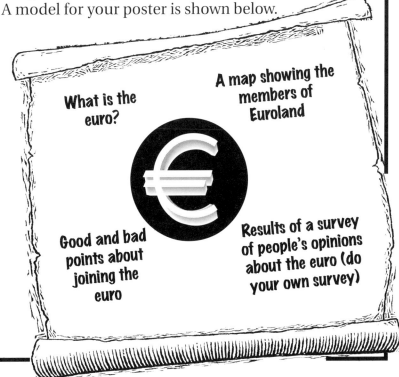

What is the euro?

A map showing the members of Euroland

Good and bad points about joining the euro

Results of a survey of people's opinions about the euro (do your own survey)

Enquiry Skills

INVESTIGATING USING A LETTER

Lindsey sent a letter to the European Union asking for information on the euro. A letter aims to get particular pieces of information. A letter must be set out properly with the following included:

- your address and the date
- the name and address of the person or organisation to whom you are writing
- tell them the reason for the letter
- ask specific questions
- thank them for their help
- sign the letter

Using a letter to investigate has some good points and some bad points.

GOOD POINTS

- You can ask exact questions.
- You can address it to a specific person who can answer your questions.
- It is cheap to send a letter.
- You may get a large amount of up-to-date information.

BAD POINTS

- The person or organisation might not answer.
- Your letter may get lost in the post.
- The information might be irrelevant.
- You might get a reply, but only months later when it is too late.

ACTIVITIES

Copy the heading: **Enquiry Skills – Investigating using a letter**

1 Why is sending a letter a good way to investigate the euro?

2 How would you find out the address of the person or organisation to send your letter?

3 Copy the statements below about using a letter. Beside each statement write down whether it is a good point or a bad point.

- You might get a reply, but only months later when it is too late.
- You can ask exact questions.
- Your letter may get lost in the post.
- The person or organisation might not answer.
- You can address it to a specific person who can answer your questions.
- It is cheap to send a letter.
- You may get a large amount of up-to-date information.
- The information might be irrelevant.

Countries which want to **join** the EU

Legend:
- EU countries
- Countries which want to join the EU

Poland – EU is considering an application for membership.

Slovakia – It has a weak economy so the EU will not let it join just now.

Hungary – EU is considering an application for membership.

Bulgaria – It has a weak economy so the EU will not let it join just now.

Czech Republic – EU is considering an application for membership.

Romania – It has a weak economy so the EU will not let it join just now.

Albania – It has a weak economy so the EU will not let it join just now.

Cyprus – It is an island split between Turkey and Greece. It has a weak economy and the political system is not stable. The EU will not let it join at the moment.

Malta – EU is considering an application for membership.

Turkey – It has a weak economy and it is not a democratic country so the EU will not let it join just now.

Map labels: SWEDEN, FINLAND, UNITED KINGDOM, DENMARK, IRELAND, NETHERLANDS, GERMANY, BELGIUM, LUXEMBOURG, FRANCE, Poland, Czech Republic, Slovakia, AUSTRIA, Hungary, Bulgaria, Romania, ITALY, SPAIN, PORTUGAL, Albania, GREECE, Turkey, Malta

ENLARGING THE EUROPEAN UNION

Countries which wish to join the European Union must satisfy three conditions. Firstly, a country must be democratic. In a democratic country the people elect the government they want. They are able to change the government if they do not like what it is doing. In a demo-cratic country, therefore, there must be regular elections.

The second condition is that the country must respect human rights. Citizens of the country must have certain freedoms and rights such as freedom of speech, right to a fair trial and freedom from ill-treatment and torture.

The third condition is that the country must have a strong economy. A country with a strong economy can contribute to the wealth of the EU and will not rely on the EU to provide handouts all the time. Poor countries will create higher unemploy-ment in the EU and will reduce the standard of living for the member countries.

ARGUMENTS FOR AND AGAINST LETTING COUNTRIES JOIN THE EUROPEAN UNION

If we let rich countries become members of the European Union we could trade with them. This would make us both richer.

With more countries in the European Union there would be less chance of fighting between countries. This would make Europe a far more stable continent.

With more countries in the European Union there would be more opportunities for people to find jobs.

Poor countries would be entitled to more aid from the European Union than they give in taxes. The poor regions in existing member countries would get less help from the European Regional Development Fund and the Common Agricultural Policy. This would make these regions poorer.

Some countries trying to join the European Union are poor and wages are low. This would attract firms to move to these countries. This would cause unemployment in existing member countries.

Poor people from the poor countries which want to join the European Union would migrate in large numbers to the richer member countries. This could cause racism and violence towards the migrants.

ACTIVITIES

Copy the heading: **Enlarging the European Union**

1 If a country wishes to join the European Union, what three conditions must it satisfy?

2 Which countries wish to join the European Union?

3 Which of these countries are most likely to be allowed to become members of the European Union?

4 Explain why the following countries might not be allowed to join the EU:
Albania; Cyprus; Slovakia; Turkey.

5 Study the statements being made by the people above. Arrange these statements under the following headings.

Arguments for letting countries join the European Union	Arguments against letting countries join the European Union